Christopher Gower was ~~~~~~~~~~~~~~
from his time as an unde~~~~~~~~~~~~~~
Nottingham University, h~~~~~~~~~~~~~~
in the capital. Prior to ordination as an Anglican priest,
he was a civil servant and for four years a police officer
in the Metropolitan Police. Since ordination in 1973 he
has worked in seven parishes and is currently Rector of
St Marylebone Parish Church in Central London. For
20 of those years since ordination he has also worked in
secular employment in local government in various
London boroughs, including in Chief Officer posts in
education, leisure and community services. He has an
MA in Pastoral Liturgy from Heythrop College,
London University and an MTh in Preaching from the
University of Wales, the first person to be awarded such
a degree. He is married with two children.

SPEAKING OF HEALING

Christopher Gower

Published in Great Britain in 2003
Society for Promoting Christian Knowledge
Holy Trinity Church
Marylebone Road
London NW1 4DU

British Library Cataloguing-in-Publication Data
A catalogue record for this book is available from the British Library

ISBN 0-281-05539-4

1 3 5 7 9 10 8 6 4 2

Typeset by WestKey Ltd, Falmouth, Cornwall
Printed in Great Britain by Bookmarque Ltd, Croydon, Surrey

Contents

Acknowledgements   ix

1 **Introduction**   1
  The context
  Healing in the Gospels
  Speaking of healing today

2 **Issues in healing**   15
  What is health?
  Healing and ageing
  The problem of evil and suffering
  Faith and healing
  Healing and evangelism
  Sickness as a punishment for sin
  Healing and the demonic
  The worshipping environment
  Evidence for healing

3 **Ways of preaching Gospel healing stories**   47
  Literal model
  Liberal model
  Metaphorical/spiritual model
  Social/community model

4 **Preaching controversial issues**   61
  Sickness as a punishment for sin
  Healing and the demonic

5 **Conclusion**   87
  'To preach and to heal'
  Literal versus liberal
  Metaphorical/spiritual model
  Social/community model
  An analogy
  Preaching the Gadarene demoniac
  Dick's story
  The eschatological dimension

  Notes   113

In memory of my parents,
gone before me marked with the sign of faith.

Acknowledgements

With grateful thanks to the Revd Dr Stephen Wright, Director of the College of Preachers, for the supervision of my MTh dissertation which forms the basis of this book, and to Jill Holmes, my secretary, for typing the manuscripts. Also, for the encouragement of my wife Carolyn who, during the writing of this book, sadly had to retire early with ill-health from being Head Teacher of a church school, which focused my mind even more on the subject of speaking about healing.

1

Introduction

The context

The idea for this book arose out of a conference that I hosted at St Marylebone Parish Church in conjunction with the College of Preachers entitled *To Preach and to Heal*, reflecting Jesus' injunction to his disciples 'to proclaim the kingdom of God and to heal' (Luke 9.2). The conference was attended by over 50 preachers and its purpose was to examine how we can use the healing stories in the Gospels to preach honestly and faithfully about healing today. That theme is explored further in this book, which I hope will be a help both to preachers and those with an interest in healing who listen to their sermons.

St Marylebone has for many years been involved in the healing ministry. It is the parish church of Harley Street with its world renowned medical community, and a number of doctors and consultants attend the church. In the church's crypt is the St Marylebone Healing and Counselling Centre run by a priest psychotherapist with a team of counsellors and psychotherapists. The crypt also houses a National Health Service medical practice, whose 8,500 patients are looked after by six doctors and a range of complementary therapists, nursing and other specialist staff. The centre was opened in 1988 by HRH Prince Charles, who has retained an interest in its work ever since, visiting again at the turn of the millennium when the Health Centre was remodelled.

As the Rector of St Marylebone I am Chaplain to seven private hospitals in the Harley Street area, including the King Edward VII's Hospital for Officers, which is used by the Royal Family. The church has regular healing services and many distinguished speakers have preached at these services over the years. St Marylebone was a natural venue, therefore, for a conference on how to preach about healing. My opening address to the conference identified some of the key problems and questions that need to be addressed when seeking to use the Gospel healing stories to preach honestly and faithfully about healing today, and these are reflected in this book.

One of the themes that kept recurring at the conference was that any preaching about healing has, of course, to be set in the context of the problem of suffering. This came home to me with some force a few years ago, on 9 December 1988 to be precise, when two things dropped through my vicarage letter box. One was a copy of the *Daily Mail*. The other was a letter from the local Pentecostal church about coming to hear Melvin Banks, one of Britain's most renowned healing evangelists, preach at a great miracle healing crusade. The letter urged one to hear Melvin Banks. It said: 'Melvin Banks, a household name throughout Britain [there's a miracle of exaggeration for a start], has been ministering the all-powerful word of God for thirty-one years. He has crusaded in twenty-one nations with

thousands of people being miraculously healed [...].
The blind have seen, the stone deaf have heard, the lame
and crippled have walked.'

On the other hand the *Daily Mail* that day carried
these front page headlines: '100,000 feared killed as
Armenian towns are destroyed by earthquake.' There
was a photograph of the devastation and then the bold
headline which read: 'The people God forgot.' It went
on to say: 'A deeply religious people, who must at times
have wondered if God had forsaken them, were last
night mourning the latest tragedy after one of the
modern world's most devastating earthquakes' – while
Melvin Banks prepared to preach about the God who
intervenes to heal at Hayes Pentecostal Church.

Any preaching about healing has to be set in the
context of the problem of suffering. Someone said,
'There is not the least use in preaching to anyone unless
you chance to catch them ill.' There's an element of
truth in that. The more vulnerable we are the more
likely we are to listen. On the other hand David Jenkins,
the former Bishop of Durham, once said that the more
one encouraged expectancy that God would heal, the
more one plunged into despair those who are not
healed. There's an element of truth in that as well. We
have all heard promises made by some preachers about
healing where they should be sued under the Trades
Descriptions Act. Preachers have an awesome responsibility. 'There are already too many horror stories of
people who have followed their preachers' encouragement to rely on faith alone, who have stopped taking
their medication or decided not to seek medical help,
and who have died as a result.'[1]

A leading Christian hospice, the Mildmay Hospital in London, recently brought together bishops and medical experts to challenge current 'healing' practice among some charismatics in which HIV/AIDS patients are encouraged to drop their medication in order to be healed. Their concern was that certain charismatic leaders were preaching that a person can only 'claim their healing' by giving up medication, which in some cases could be life-saving drugs. At the Mildmay Hospital one patient who had been helped back to health through care, medicine and prayer subsequently attended a charismatic healing service and was told to discontinue their treatment. While remaining well for a while, their condition then deteriorated and the person died. The Bishop of Chelmsford commented at the time that some charismatic Christians wrongly tried to create a dichotomy between medicine and prayer, for Jesus is our healer whether through medicine, or prayer or both. Certainly the partnership between religion and medicine is an important one.

I am reminded of a hospital chaplain telling the following supposedly true story at a healing service at St Marylebone of the partnership between priest and doctor in North Wales. A parson and doctor were sitting in the bedroom of a dying man, talking with the man's wife. After a while the priest got up from his chair, looked closely at the dying man and commented, 'I don't think it will be long now.' The doctor replied, 'Yes, it won't be long.' A few minutes later the priest got up again from his chair, went over to the bed and remarked, 'I think he's gone.' With that the doctor got up and looked at the man and said, 'Yes, he's gone.'

Suddenly the old man sat up in bed and exclaimed, 'Oh no I haven't!' His wife replied, 'Now, now, my dear, parson and doctor know best' – the partnership of religion and medicine.

In April 2001 ITV showed a documentary entitled *Miracles*.[2] Its ostensible subject matter was an examination of the preaching ministries of Benny Hinn and Reinhard Bonnke, two of the world's most successful Christian healers. It showed them preaching a direct link between a person's level of faith and the chance of miraculous healing. As the review of the programme in the *Church Times* put it: 'But we also saw the heartbreaking scenes behind the stage of those with conditions quite unsusceptible to the phenomena. Showing us a boy with brain damage brought by his mother to every rally for fifteen years, the commentator asked, "What must it feel like to hear again and again that God has the power to heal you, but chooses not to?" ' The *Church Times* review stated, 'These are the questions that people of faith need to confront, that should jolt us out of the comforting and easy theologies so often peddled in the name of Christianity.' The review of the programme concluded: 'It ended positively, providing some sort of answer: at Lourdes, where the authorities have claimed fewer miraculous cures in the shrine's history than Bonnke or Hinn claim in a single night. Millions come to experience the real miracle of finding meaning, by experiencing love which is both human and divine, in suffering and death.'[3]

The conference at St Marylebone provided an opportunity for the participants to reflect on what theologies undergird the preaching of healing texts found in the

Gospel narratives. Our understanding of the Bible and our theology about God have a strong influence on our interpretation of the healing narratives for homiletics. What connections do we make between the biblical texts and our contemporary situations?

A further question that needs to be asked is: 'What effect does our preaching have on people who live with disabilities today?' – because the manner in which preachers expound these texts can be oppressive to those who have disabilities. As the television programme said: 'What must it feel like to hear again and again that God has the power to heal, but chooses not to?' In that television programme we heard Hinn say slowly and with great power and emotion: 'All things are possible to him that believeth. All things are possible to him that believeth. All things. Every need. Every prayer. All things are possible. All you have to do is to believe, because everything is possible with God.'

How can we preach honestly and faithfully about healing today? As Hinn does? So often preachers like this can imply, however unintentionally, that disability is a punishment for lack of faith or for sin. Even when we preach healing texts metaphorically – when we talk of being blind to seeing the truth or deaf to hearing the word of God – what effect does our preaching have on those who live with disabilities today? Perhaps the underlying question we need to ask is: 'What is the meaning of healing in the lives of people with sickness and disability today?' Here then are some of the issues that I seek to address in this book. In such a short book on a rather complex subject it is, of course, only possible to deal briefly with the many different aspects of healing as they relate to preaching.

Healing in the Gospels

This book is primarily about preaching the healing stories in the Gospels. What are we to make of such stories? Wright, in commenting on Jesus' 'mighty works', states: 'Recent history has been coming to the conclusion that we can only explain the evidence before us if we reckon that Jesus did indeed perform deeds for which there was at the time, and may well be still, no obvious "naturalistic" explanation.'[4]

But what did Jesus think he was doing and why? What also did his healings mean to the recipients of them and also to the Gospel writers who recounted these stories? In reading the Gospels we can see that Jesus' healing miracles brought physical health, wholeness and peace. Their effects also brought sufferers back into membership of the community of the people of God, where previously they had been excluded because of their sickness or whatever.[5]

For the Gospel writers, and indeed for Jesus himself, these mighty works were not supernatural displays of power for their own sake, but signs of the physical inauguration of God's kingdom whereby he comes in power to save and to heal. The heart of Jesus' message is the preaching of the kingdom of God. This kingdom is not a realm but a reign, the dynamic reign and rule of God. Jesus spoke paradoxically of this kingdom, as though it was something which was both in the future and also a present reality.

Jesus incorporated into his preaching of God's kingdom the symbol, as Meier puts it, 'of the definitive coming of God in the near future to bring the present state of things to an end and to establish his full and unimpeded rule over the world in general and Israel in particular. Although the urgent tone of Jesus' message emphasised the imminence of the kingdom's arrival, Jesus [...] did not set any timetable for the kingdom's appearance.'[6]

This eschatological kingdom that Jesus preached about will result in the reversal of all unjust oppression and suffering and bestow upon the people of God the blessings of the kingdom which will transcend death itself. Although God is the Lord of history, the world will continue to witness a conflict between God's kingdom and the hostile opposing forces of the realm of evil which seek to frustrate God's rule. The perfect realization and establishment of God's kingly rule will only finally be accomplished by a supernatural world-transforming future act of God which will bring about a restored creation. 'This future, transcendent salvation was an essential part of Jesus' proclamation of the kingdom.'[7]

Paradoxically, however, not everything in Jesus' message and deeds could be explained simply in terms of the future. 'A number of sayings and actions of Jesus argue strongly for the view that Jesus spoke of the kingdom as already present in some way or to some degree in his ministry.'[8] He appears to claim that through his miraculous works of healing and exorcism the kingdom of God has already become present. In both word and deed Jesus made God's kingdom a present reality.

This breaking-in of the kingdom can also be seen in his battle with Satan, particularly in the case of his exorcisms and the healing of those whose conditions were attributed to evil spirits. An example is the healing of a demoniac who was blind and mute in Luke 11.20 (cf. Matthew 12.28) where Jesus says: 'If it is by the finger of God that I cast out the demons, then the kingdom of God has come to you.'

We see, therefore, that God's kingdom, 'which will appear as an apocalyptic act at the end of the age, has already come into human history in the person and mission of Jesus to overcome evil, to deliver men from its power, and to bring them into the blessings of God's reign'.[9] The kingdom of God, the dynamic rule of God, has invaded human history in the person and mission of Jesus, although its consummation still awaits the age to come at the end of history.

The evangelists wrote up the stories of Jesus' healings in their Gospels at a time when some healing continued to take place in the early Church, according to the book of Acts. The question is whether they were simply recording what Jesus had done or whether they were also intending to say that this is a model of what we are supposed to be doing today, as a continuation of Jesus' activity in the world. This is an important issue that will be taken up later in this book.

Speaking of healing today

The British Government has provided for a substantial increase in funding for the Health Service over the next few years. Indeed, politicians operate on the assumption

once voiced by Nigel Lawson, a former Chancellor of
the Exchequer, that the National Health Service is the
British religion. There is no doubt that health is one of
the most important subjects occupying modern society
at the beginning of this new millennium, as people
search for a lifestyle which offers the alluring elixir of a
long and healthy life.

Likewise, preaching about healing is of vital importance and significance today, especially when one
considers the extent of the healing narratives in the
Gospels and the frequency with which such stories
therefore occur in church lectionaries for preaching
purposes. Over 38 per cent of the narrative verses in the
Gospels (484 verses) are devoted to describing Jesus'
healing miracles. The attention given to Jesus' healing
ministry is far greater than any other subject. Indeed, 40
per cent of Mark's Gospel, which is probably the earliest
Gospel, is taken up with healing stories. The Gospels
record 38 incidents of healing: 26 individuals and 12
groups or summaries of larger numbers of people. No
wonder William Temple said: 'You cannot read the
gospels and cut out the ministry of healing without
tearing them to ribbons.'[10]

'In the New Testament Jesus' healings are inextricably linked with his preaching of the gospel of the
kingdom of God – the good news is the promise of
wholeness for humanity.'[11] We see in the Gospels Jesus
combining healing with the proclamation of the
kingdom of God, which people were challenged to
respond to and experience. The healings are not to be
seen as all-important features in themselves. The
Gospel writers placed the healing activities of Jesus

within a preaching framework. Likewise his followers were sent out 'to proclaim the kingdom of God and to heal' (Luke 9.2). In the longer ending of Mark's Gospel and in the Acts of the Apostles there are several references to the fact that signs such as healing accompanied and confirmed the preaching of the gospel in the early Church.

The report *A Time to Heal* states that 'the healing ministry is one of the greatest opportunities the Church has today for sharing the gospel'.[12] The rapid development of the healing ministry in the contemporary Church can be seen from the results of the English Church Attendance Survey published in *The Church of England Newspaper* on 13 July 2001. Nearly half (44 per cent) of all Church of England churches have some kind of healing service (81 per cent of Pentecostal churches). The sermon, of course, plays a vitally important part in a healing service. However, alongside this growth in the healing ministry, there needs to take place considerable theological reflection. 'The development of a theology of suffering as well as a theology of wholeness must be placed higher up the agenda of important issues to be tackled by Christians.'[13]

Having established the crucial importance of my subject in this introductory chapter, I now set out what I aim to do in this study. Chapter 2 will be taken up with exploring a range of issues connected with the healing ministry that impact upon our preaching. These issues include the question 'What is health?' (with reference also to ageing and healing), the apologetic task of theodicy relating to the problem of evil and suffering, the links between faith and healing miracles and between healing and evangelism, the seeing of sickness as a punishment for sin, and the realm of healing and the demonic. No study on preaching and healing would be complete without looking at the worshipping environment in which it is set and the reaction of the hearers – those who have to listen to sermons on the subject. Nor can we conclude our study without looking at contemporary evidence for healing, which must affect our expectations and to some extent condition how we preach about healing.

Chapter 3 will critique various models or ways of preaching about healing, of which I have identified four:

1　A literal model which accepts that Jesus healed people and which may or may not include expectations that we should seek such physical healing today

2　A liberal model which is suspicious of any kind of supernatural miraculous healings

3　A metaphorical/spiritual model which may or may not accept healing miracles, but which applies the texts in other ways by dealing with spiritual realities arising from them

4　A model which is more concerned with the social/community implications and dimensions of healing

These models are not all mutually exclusive, of course. Our expectations, or lack of them, concerning healing will obviously influence which model we preachers adopt and the way we preach and minister to the sick.

Chapter 4 will examine the application of these models to two of the key issues identified in Chapter 2, those which are possibly the most controversial with respect to the healing narratives in the Gospels – sickness as a punishment for sin and healing and the demonic. The final chapter summarizes the insights and discoveries thrown up by this study, which hopefully will assist us to preach honestly and faithfully about healing when we use the healing stories in the Gospels today.

2

Issues in healing

What is health?

In present-day usage the word 'health' is usually associated with the efficient functioning of the body and 'healing' with recovery from illness, although these words can have wider connotations. A biblical understanding of health involves a close relationship between healing, wholeness and salvation. Indeed, the New Testament word for salvation (*sozo*) conveys the idea of soundness of health in body, mind and spirit. Christian healing is not, therefore, just about recovery from physical illness. It is also about our mental well-being which comes from a right ordering of our inner life. It includes the health of our relationships with other people and above all our relationship with God, the source of all life and health. Health, therefore, is a state of complete physical, mental, social and spiritual well-being. Preaching on healing, if it is to be balanced, needs to reflect these different aspects of wholeness.

However, it should be recognized that wholeness inevitably involves the acceptance of limitations if it is not to be utopian, for we are all limited in one way or another. This is particularly true of the disabled. For some 'wholeness may have to be experienced within the reality of sickness of some kind. People do not have to get up out of their wheelchairs to show the healing power and presence of God at work in their lives.'[1] Sermons need to reflect such truth.

A good example of this is a sermon preached at a healing service at St Marylebone in which the following story made a profound impression on the congregation. The visiting preacher spoke of the world-renowned violinist Itzhak Perlman, who was stricken with polio as a child. In 1994 he gave a concert in New York. Simply getting on to the stage with heavy braces on both legs and walking with the aid of crutches was no small achievement. He had only played a few bars when one of the strings on his violin broke. He signalled for the conductor to begin again and, as the orchestra struck up, he recomposed the piece of music in his head and played the entire composition perfectly with incredible power and passion on just the three strings he had left. When he had finished there was an awesome silence, following which the entire audience rose and cheered wildly. When the applause had died down Perlman said humbly, 'You know, sometimes it is the artist's task to find out how much music you can still make with what you have left.' A newspaper music critic wrote this the next day: 'Perhaps this is the way of life for all of us: to make music, at first with all we have, and then, when that is no longer possible, to make music with what we have left.'

Health and wholeness, of course, extend beyond the individual's need for health to the corporate need for a healthy community. How can we bring God's healing to a sick society? What are the social, moral, economic and environmental issues we need to address in our sermons which give rise to the wider causes of ill health?

There are many different aspects to lack of health. Health is an environmental issue because damage to the environment can impair our health. This gives rise to an economic issue, because there is inevitably conflict involved in one person's pollution being another person's livelihood. Health is also a justice issue for poverty is probably the main cause of disease. So it is also a political issue. The politics of health is about the haves and the have-nots, for the poor have less access to medical facilities. Health is also a peace issue, for one sees the results of the various civil wars around the world and the tragic results of terrorist warfare. All forms of violence have their effects on health.

All these matters need to be addressed in our preaching. Unfortunately today religion has been relegated to the private sphere, but we cannot keep politics, health and social issues out of the pulpit. As Henry Scott Holland put it, 'The more you believe in the incarnation, the more you care about drains.'[2] Or as former US President Eisenhower said: 'Every gun that is made, every warship launched, every rocket fired, signifies, in a final sense, a theft from those who hunger and are not fed, from those who are cold and are not clothed.'[3] Jesus was concerned to preach about the plight of these people in the Gospels (Matthew 25.31–46; Luke 4.16–21). Should not those who preach in his name be equally so?

Healing and ageing

We all want to live longer but nobody wants to grow old. Scientists tell us that many babies born today can expect to live to a hundred. The length of our lives depends to some extent on lifestyle and how we treat our bodies through life. There is also some truth in the adage 'we are what we eat.' The world is obsessed with perpetual youth. Many middle-aged people dread the thought of growing old, let alone of death itself. In the near future a quarter of the population of this country will be over 60. An ageing population has implications for society on a scale previously unheard of and these will no doubt feature in our sermons. Issues related to ageing will take a higher priority, but many who live longer will also suffer many more years of ill health. According to figures published in 2002 by the Office for National Statistics, while people in England are living longer they are likely to suffer on average almost ten years of ill health in their later years. The search for healing, therefore, will gather momentum, for an increase in longevity without quality of life is an empty prize. Although we all seek immortality, death is inevitable and there has to be a point where a line is drawn between length of life and quality of life.

Ageing is inevitably characterized by physical and mental decline and we have to find ways of coping with it. Sensitive preaching to the elderly, particularly at services in residential homes, can help people face this. Medical advances have done much to improve an elderly person's quality of life, but are unable to cure such 'diseases' as loneliness and despair. This is where the Church has an important part to play in providing fellowship and care. Part of its ministry is to help people 'come to terms with the different stages in their lives and the ways in which their need for healing may change'.[4]

We certainly preach to more elderly congregations nowadays and need to take account of this. There are more elderly people in society now than ever before and churchgoers tend to be from an older age range in any case. But are elderly people too old to receive healing? What do we tell them from the pulpit about the hope of healing? From the healing miracles in the Gospels we are unable to tell whether Jesus ever healed an elderly person. Perhaps the man at the pool of Beth-zatha who had been ill for 38 years could be numbered among the elderly of his day and possibly Lazarus was advanced in years when Jesus raised him from the dead. Certainly today we hear reports of older people allegedly being healed through prayer. An article in the *Church Times* recorded how the Bishop of Kimberley and Kuruman in South Africa prayed for an 84-year-old man and his wife who were both healed of blindness. The next day another elderly woman was also healed of blindness. The Bishop stated, 'These were all people whose lack of sight would be accounted for by their advanced age. But with the Lord it's never too late.'[5]

However, when we preach about healing, particularly at healing services, are we really offering the hope of God reversing the ageing process and healing people of age-related degenerative conditions such as arthritis, enlarged prostates, etc.? We must be careful of building false expectations, while at the same time not limiting God. When I talked about healing and ageing to a lay reader colleague of mine at St Marylebone who is a professor and the dean of a university medical school, he replied: 'Now there's a contradiction!' Similarly, when I asked a doctor, who is a committed Christian, what she thought about the divine healing of age-related conditions, she replied: 'I think God is realistic.'

Of course, following the Human Genome Project and the decoding of the human genetic code, medical science may in future produce ways to slow down the ageing process and cure diseases like Alzheimer's, Parkinson's, diabetes and cancer. As former US President Clinton remarked: 'It is conceivable that our children's children will know the word "cancer" only as a constellation of stars.' Meanwhile it is not unknown today to hear of the very rich trying to prolong life by choosing to have their bodies deep frozen when they die, in anticipation of clinical advances that will be able to cure terminal disease when they are unfrozen again at some future date.

As we get older, however, we have to come to terms with our own mortality. There inevitably comes a time for a person to die. For such people preaching a false hope of healing brings unnecessary pain and deflects attention from trusting God for eternal life. Ours is a culture in which death is the great unmentionable, for the dying remind us of how our own story will one day end.

'Whenever we speak of healing, I think we must also think (and maybe speak) of death, because death is the *ultimate healing*.'[6] Sometimes when we preach we have to preach on healing the dying, teaching people on the journey towards death how to live life to the full what-ever their physical condition, and to hear the voice of God in the midst of their fears, anger and dependency. It has been said that God gave us a fear of death as part of our equipment for living; so we encourage people from the pulpit to live whatever time is left earnestly, with their eyes fixed on eternity and the hope of resurrection, for the best is yet to be.

Perhaps sermons which refer to ageing should reflect the sentiments conveyed in this 'prayer for growing old' by an unknown author:

> Eternal God, I thank you that I am growing old. It is a privilege that many have been denied. Awareness of this mercy gives fresh wonder to every day [...]. I thank you for the joys I can now grasp because age has prised my fingers loose from trivial things – for simpler life; for unhurried moments to nourish faith on thoughts of your past mercies; for sacred instants when all things that once seemed disjointed fall into place and the sad things of earth are swallowed up in holy joy. Heavenly Father, grant us awareness of the beauties of life's autumn, a time of fulfilment and harvest. May age be seen as part of your design for the world and for us, so that the years may rest less like a burden and more like a benediction. Spare us from the self-pity that shrivels the soul. Though our wrinkles multiply and bodies tire, may there be no withering of our spirit [...]. Though our money may be limited, let us be spendthrifts with love [...]. And grant us daily some moments living on tiptoes, lured by the eternal city just beyond the hills of time.

The problem of evil and suffering

From the theological point of view health and sickness require meaning. They need to be interpreted as part of human experience. Is there meaning in human suffering and where does God stand in relation to it? The justification of God's ways in the face of the problem of evil and suffering and his relationship with it is what is known as theodicy and is vital to our preaching about healing. As Tull points out: 'A parishioner who is critically ill may raise a theological question to her pastor: "What did I do to deserve this?" A congregation deserves to know how its minister will answer such a question – not from a bedside, but from the pulpit, drawing upon the biblical witness.'[7]

The prevailing theodicy of Jesus' day was that sickness was understood to be caused by human sinfulness, which I deal with in Chapter 4. However, in John 9 and Luke 13 it would appear that Jesus would have us reject this notion. Indeed, the gospel witness is of a Jesus who did not himself escape the experience of suffering and death in agony on a cross.

Given Jesus' battles with the evil one, it is also easy to shift responsibility for suffering on to the Devil, as some preachers are inclined to do. Wimber, for example, states: 'This raises the question of why the righteous suffer. The answer to this, in part, is that we have been thrust into a war with Satan and, as in any war, there are casualties.'[8] Ultimately, however, the Devil is no answer to the problem of the origin of evil and suffering because God is the source of the created order that includes the Devil, whom he has allowed to create such havoc.

Mainstream Christian theodicy has been built upon the Augustinian tradition, which sees suffering as a direct consequence of human sin.[9] God created a perfect world, and the evil and suffering in it are the consequences of Adam's sin which has infected the entire human race (commonly known as the 'Fall of Man'). Many are now unable to see this as authentic history, however, for science has shown that suffering existed long before the first human beings appeared. Some have posited a mythological pre-mundane 'fall of angels' as responsible, but this is hardly a more adequate explanation of evil, for how did perfect humans or angels fall in the first place in a perfect environment?

Another tradition within Christian thinking, however, sees the origin of evil and suffering in more evolutionary terms. Instead of God creating humans in a finished state of perfection, this Irenaean tradition sees humanity as still in the process of creation. This process of development allows room for the theory that creation, because it is not yet perfected, is a place of suffering. From this Christian thinkers, such as Hick for example, have developed a theodicy which sees this world as a place of 'soul making' in which human personality may be fashioned towards the pattern of Christ. The value of a world of suffering and evil is to be judged primarily as to whether it is suitable for this purpose. Certainly, development of moral character could not take place in a hedonistic pain-free paradise which offered no real challenges.

Theodicy arguments usually begin by identifying two types of evil – moral evil (wilful bad actions such as the Holocaust) and physical evil (disease, earthquake, disasters, etc.). The 'free will defence' is commonly used in relation to moral evil. As Polkinghorne describes this: 'It claims that it is better for creation to contain freely choosing persons, however disastrous some of their choices may prove to be, than to be populated with perfectly programmed automata.'[10] We were not created puppets or robots. We were created real people with freedom of choice and so there is the possibility of us rejecting God and spoiling our lives and the world in which we live.

The second type of evil is physical evil. The recently published World Disaster Report stated that, in the year 2000, avalanches, landslides, droughts, floods, famine, windstorms, earthquakes and other natural disasters seriously affected 256 million people. Polkinghorne has suggested that there is an analogous 'free-process defence' in relation to physical evil – 'A world allowed to make itself through the evolutionary exploration of its potentiality is a better world than one produced ready-made by divine fiat.'[11] God did not simply make the world; he made the world make itself. He has given everything in it a life of its own and woven the universe through the free interplay of millions of forces. This means that various accidents, malfunctions, possibilities of terminal illness and suffering inevitably arise.

A belief in God's providential care of the world and individuals within it lies at the heart of the Christian faith. The Gospel narrative accounts of the life of Jesus and of his healing ministry assume such an understanding of God's providential intervention. Fundamentalist preachers take this to the extreme by portraying a God who is in tight control of everything that happens in the world, even though the evidence of the created order seems to rule out such totalitarianism. Many people find it very difficult to let go of the belief that God is somehow in control of this universe at every step of the way. For others, however, the idea of an all-powerful God needs to be refined.

The classic case against such a God concerns the Christian belief that God is all-powerful and all-good. If he is all-powerful he must be able to abolish evil and suffering, unless he does not want to, then he cannot be all-good. Most theologians have therefore moved towards the view that there are constraints on divine action in the world. For example, Ward argues: 'The nature of any universe that God wills is such that there will be definite constraints on the actions of a God who acts through the persuasion of love rather than through irresistible power.'[12] He suggests that we reject the idea that God can do absolutely anything at all. This is directly the opposite of the approach taken by Hinn, quoted in my introduction, who preaches a healing God for whom all things are possible if we believe. Ward is still able, however, to call God 'omnipotent' because no one has greater power than God who is the source of all other beings. The free will argument means that a great deal of suffering is brought about by evil choices that are divinely unpreventable. God does not intend this evil, but cannot prevent it as long as he continues to will freedom. His hands are tied and his freedom of action restricted. He can only suffer with us as our pain becomes his pain.

A productive line in preaching about healing in the face of the issues raised by theodicy is indicated by Black: 'Disability is a part of everyday existence for millions of people and their loved ones in this world. Does God cause it to happen? No. This does not mean, however, that God is not present for us in the midst of it, willing each person's well-being even in the situation of permanent disability.'[13] She lays great stress on God upholding us in the midst of devastations, sufferings, frustrations and disabilities, and of him providing transforming opportunities. This is a helpful approach for preaching on the subject of theodicy. 'God works to transform our lives at every moment, in all our various circumstances, through the power of love. God wills the well-being that is possible for each one of us. These transformations are not necessarily the kind that we recognize as miraculous, although some clearly are. The possibility of transformation is present at every moment of our lives.'[14]

Classical theodicies remain largely irrelevant for preaching purposes for they 'leave God untouched by suffering or responsibility and do not answer pastoral need'.[15] Indeed, sermons on theodicy can often be more concerned with defending the integrity of God who allows such suffering, than saying anything helpful to alleviate the sufferers' pain and distress. No theodicy argument has ever produced a satisfactory explanation for the problem of evil and suffering and probably never will, for 'we do not know why the creator allowed suffering and death to enter into his creation'.[16]

Faith and healing

What is faith? The basic meaning of faith in the Gospels equates it with belief and trust in the person of Jesus, his mission and his ability and willingness to grant healing. Faith is a common ingredient in the Gospel healing accounts, as can be seen from the number of narratives containing such phrases as 'Let it be done to you according to your faith' and 'Your faith has made you well.'

Some healings are in response to the sick person's faith, e.g. Matthew 9.22; 9.28; Mark 5.34; 10.52; Luke 17.19; 18.42. There are other occasions, however, where only the faith of the relatives or friends is mentioned, e.g. Matthew 8.13; 15.28; Mark 2.5; 9.24; Luke 7.9. In Mark 6.1–6 and the Matthean equivalent, when Jesus visited his own home town, the explanation for meagre results of healing was the people's lack of faith. However, in some healing narratives no faith seems to be shown, either by the one healed or by anyone else except Jesus, e.g. Mark 7.31–37; Luke 7.11–17; 13.10–17; 14.1–6; 22.49–51; John 5.2–47; 11.2–44.

Nevertheless we can see that faith is a common ingredient in a number of Gospel healing narratives. It is also a live issue for preachers in the contemporary Church. Today, the issue of faith in relation to healing and how to preach it is a complex one. There are evangelists who stress that it is only through faith that God releases his power to heal. Many involved in the healing ministry see Jesus' own healing ministry as a paradigm for contemporary Christians to follow and in preaching they emphasize the importance of faith, as Jesus did on occasions. MacNutt, referring to lack of faith, comments: 'Part of the present crisis of faith is, I think, related to a basic lack of confidence in prayer. Some preaching, emphasizing caution and stressing that God often says no, has contributed to this lack of hope and faith.'[17]

However, MacNutt cautions: 'If the only factor the evangelist stresses is, Do you have the faith to be healed? then people accept the converse, If I am not healed it is because my faith is weak. Simplistic preaching causes guilt in those who are not healed and increases resistance in those who are skeptical about the very possibility of healing.'[18] The preaching of Hinn in the television documentary referred to in my introduction is a classic example of this.

A Time to Heal warns: 'The idea that healing is just a matter of faith is very misleading. It leads to cruel advice such as, "You'll be healed if you have faith" (implying that if you're not healed it's your fault!). This is completely contrary to the teaching of the New Testament.'[19] This emphasis on faith can have the effect of making Jesus a servant of such a faith, whereby he can be manipulated and coerced into healing through it. This is a travesty of the gospel.

Those who hold the view that lack of healing is indicative of lack of faith do so on the premise that Jesus' healing ministry can be emulated today and his healing made available now to all believers. Warrington states, however: 'Rather than assume that sufferers may be obstructing Jesus' desire to heal, it is more appropriate to question the premise that suggests Jesus' healing ministry may be replicated in our time.'[20] The scale of Jesus' healing ministry was unique; we cannot replicate it. Preachers who lay great stress on faith to be healed also tend to set up an artificial opposition between medicine and faith. The hearer can therefore be torn between believing in the doctors, or in the preacher who claims to speak with the authority of God.

A good example of this can be seen in the following extract from a faith-inspiring sermon entitled *Hold on, change is coming*, preached by Matthew Ashimolowo, Senior Pastor of the Kingsway International Christian Centre in London, which has a congregation of over 7,000 people and a significant healing ministry:

> The X-ray report is back and it confirms what the doctor said. Hold on because a change is coming. The doctor's X-ray is not the final word. It is a fact that they found what they wanted to find, but it is not the truth that you will not be healed. Facts and truth are not the same. Truth erases facts. It's a fact there is a sickness, which is not the truth that you will not be cured. The truth says 'for I am the Lord that healeth thee.' The truth says 'I will not allow any of the diseases of Egypt to rise and to be upon you' (Exodus 15.26) ... Hold on, your change is coming.

The medical prognosis may not be the last word, but there is a danger of setting medicine and faith in opposition to each other.

Black is concerned about the effect preaching an emphasis on faith in healing has on those with disabilities, that if people would believe more fully they would be cured. She says:

> Today, the issue of faith in relation to healing is a complicated one. On the one hand, there is no doubt that the faith of persons with disabilities sustains many in their daily existence and is a healing element in their lives. On the other hand, to judge a person's faith (either what the person believes or the degree to which the person believes) and to make physical cure the criteria of that judgment is to erect barriers between persons with disabilities and God – to destroy faith.[21]

Black also points out the problem that 'there are some disabilities, such as an amputated leg, that cannot be "cured" no matter how faithful one is'.[22] Buchanan comments in similar vein: 'When the black death killed a third of Europe in 1348, believers died alongside the doubting and probably at no different rate from them.'[23] It is wiser to suggest that 'we cannot dogmatize about the causal connection between personal faith and a recovery from particular bodily ailments'.[24] Although many have found faith to be a vital ingredient in healing, preachers need to encourage this in a balanced way when preaching Gospel healing texts, recognizing that Jesus' healing ministry was unique.

Healing and evangelism

Wimber claims that in 21 out of the 26 healings carried out by Jesus there was either an evangelistic setting or result.[25] He sees Jesus' public ministry as having two elements: proclamation of the good news of the kingdom of God and demonstration of its power through healing the sick, etc. *A Time to Heal* comments that 'the mission of the Church, therefore, is nothing less than to continue Jesus' own mission'.[26] The report states:

> After Pentecost the apostles and their followers knew they had been sent out 'to proclaim the kingdom of God and to heal' (Luke 9.2). They believed they were not on their own: the Lord was working with them and would confirm their message by the signs that accompanied it (Mark 16.20). Luke recorded that, having tasted opposition for the first time, they prayed: 'Lord, grant to your servants to speak your word with all boldness, while you stretch out your hand to heal, and signs and wonders are performed through the name of your holy servant Jesus' (Acts 4.29–30).[27]

During the apostolic era the link between preaching and healing helped to account for some of the remarkable growth of Christianity during the first hundred years or so of the Church. Parker and Lawrence claim that we weaken the gospel message if instead of holding together teaching, healing and proclaiming the good news we concentrate on just one of its parts. They comment that when we engage in mission 'we cannot break it down into compartments, whereby we may on one occasion preach the gospel and on another address the subject of healing'.[28]

Wimber remarks that 'Healing aids evangelism. It is a "gospel advancer".'[29] He argues consistently that signs and wonders are more likely to impress non-believers and convert them. *A Time to Heal* suggests that 'the healing ministry is one of the greatest opportunities the Church has today for sharing the gospel'.[30] It is the gospel preached with the hope of healing.

Skinner speaks of the word of God being released as a healing word. It is 'evangelistic preaching in which we minister to the depths of human pain, such as fear, loneliness, rejection, failure'.[31] Again he states: 'Our evangelism needs to have a contextualized depth to it so that these needs are addressed by the gospel message in a way that is actually dealing with the real problems faced. In my experience some people put over the gospel message in very superficial ways which fail to address these deeply felt needs.'[32] Skinner warns, however, that it is possible to lean too far in the opposite direction in the preaching of a 'needs-centred' gospel which focuses too much on the person rather than God.

There are others who do not find in Jesus' great commission in Matthew 28 the Church being sent out to heal as well as to preach. They note that Jesus rejected the temptation to work miracles to seduce people into believing in him. They also draw attention to Jesus' reticence towards people publicizing his healings in the Gospel narratives. Hacker comments: 'He [Jesus] seems too to have frequently forbidden people to publicize the healings that they had received. All this should at least make us cautious about trying to use the healing ministry as part of any missionary strategy.'[33]

Dr Peter May writes in an issue of the journal *Healing and Wholeness*: 'It is commonly and wrongly supposed that the Church was sent to preach and to heal, as though these were two equal and different parts of the same mandate. We need to read again the terms of the Great Commission as given by the resurrected Christ and recorded at the end of the gospel narratives.'[34] While it is true that the commission in Matthew 28 does not include the command to heal, the longer ending in Mark (16.9–20) suggests otherwise. That said, however, this ending was probably not written by Mark, for it is not included in the earliest manuscripts, but appears to have been added later in an attempt to complete his Gospel.

Sickness as a punishment for sin

In Jesus' day Jews saw a link between sin and sickness, that physical problems were the result of one's sins. Wimber goes as far as to say: 'Almost every illness recorded in the Old Testament was a result of sin and disobedience.'[35] Also, 'The New Testament shows that healing is associated with repentance from sin and conflict with Satan. Health is frequently determined by individual righteousness or sin.'[36]

Black comments: 'The connection between sin and disease/disability that has emerged in the preaching of the healing texts has created a theological perspective that continues to permeate many of our churches today.'[37] Certainly contemporary preachers involved in a ministry of healing stress the importance of forgiveness of sins in healing. Wimber writes: 'Frequently I pray for people with a physical ailment who, I discover, have serious sin in their lives. After they confess and repent of their sin, the physical condition disappears.'[38] Again MacNutt remarks: 'The first and deepest kind of healing that Christ brings is the forgiveness of sins. [...] What I have come to see, though, is how intimately the forgiveness of sins is connected with bodily and emotional healing.'[39]

Lawrence asks: 'How important is forgiveness in the ministry of Christian healing? Its importance can hardly be overestimated. It is often an element in the healing of the body. It is always involved in the healing of the spirit. It is at the heart of Christian healing because it is at the heart of the gospel itself.'[40] *A Time to Heal* comments: 'To be released from the power of sin is healing.'[41]

Certainly medically it can be seen that psychological guilt can produce physical distress. Of course some sickness can serve a higher purpose. As MacNutt points out: 'Sometimes it serves to chastise us or to bring us to our senses. At other times, it may turn us around and redirect our lives into a better course.'[42] This theme is developed outside the Gospels by the writer to the Hebrews (Hebrews 12.1–12).

We can see from the New Testament texts that there were two occasions on which Jesus appeared to heal by proclaiming the forgiveness of sins – the healing of the paralytic (Mark 2) and the man at the pool of Beth-zatha (John 5). Here Jesus may be acknowledging an interrelationship between sickness and sin. However in John 9 Jesus went against the popular belief of his day that sickness and sin were related. To the theological issue 'Is blindness caused by sin?' Jesus denied there being a direct link between the man's blindness and his sins or those of his parents. But no alternative explanation was given for the origin of suffering to help us with our preaching. Jesus merely pointed out that the healing was an opportunity to give glory to God. With regard to Mark 2.5b–10, many scholars believe that the controversy over the forgiveness of sins is a later addition by the early Church to the older healing story. If this is the case, it throws into doubt the validity of the claims of those who preach this text as justification for the theology that sin is the cause of disability.

A Time to Heal, in speaking of ministering to the sick, cautions: 'Care should be taken, of course, not to give the impression that ill health is caused by personal sin, still less that it is a divine punishment.'[43] Elsewhere the report states: 'It is unkind even to hint to an individual that his own particular sickness is the result of his or her personal sin.'[44]

All this is very different from the theology expressed in the 'Order for the Visitation of the Sick' in The Book of Common Prayer, which regards sickness as 'God's visitation', 'the chastisement of the Lord' and 'our heavenly Father's correction'. Is not this a pre-scientific view of a world where God is directly in control of what happens, determining the weather, sending sickness so that every infection is a divine visitation? This raises the question: 'How, in fact, does God act in relation to his world?' Does he act directly in this way? Hacker comments: 'The short answer is of course that we do not know.'[45] That means, he says, 'that we cannot rule out that in some sense and on some occasions he does "send" sickness, though if he does it can only be in accord with his nature as a loving Father who has a care for all his children'.[46] Hacker is of the opinion that it is more a matter of God allowing sickness and nature to take their course and of allowing our own sin to bring its own disaster upon us.

Black indignantly states: 'To preach that the reason people get the flu is because God is angry with them, let alone to put forth the notion that once the flu is gone God has forgiven our sins, is beyond absurd.'[47] Black does not deny that there is a relationship between sin and sickness, but is more concerned to see illness as sometimes caused by sins that have been committed *against* a person, or perhaps inflicted upon themselves. She states: 'To continue to preach that disability is caused by the sins of the person who *has* the disability is to deny both the physical and the psychological causes of disability – namely, sins *against* rather than sins *by* the person with the disability.'[48]

There are still other variations of the belief that sickness is a punishment for sin. These include those who preach that illnesses such as AIDS are a judgement of God on our permissive society, or that some suffering today is the direct causal effect of the sins and iniquities of a previous generation. The latter may have been true of those children who suffered as a result of the Aberfan disaster in Wales in the 1960s when a coal waste tip slid on to a school. However, it is much more difficult to believe, for example, that a child is born with a disability because of the sins of its parents.

A Time to Heal concludes: 'Sinful attitudes and actions can contribute towards or cause much sickness and suffering, selfishness, abuse, carelessness or neglect on the part of the community, or of individuals. [...] In this sense, then, we can say there is often a general connection between suffering and sin.'[49] Otherwise it is unwise to dogmatize in our preaching on the relationship between the two.

Healing and the demonic

The demonic is a controversial subject, which fits into the broader scene of healing in terms of deliverance from evil. The Gospels (and indeed the entire canon of scripture) do not account for the origin of Satan or evil spirits. The synoptic Gospels portray Jesus healing and casting out demons or unclean spirits on many occasions. John's Gospel, however, does not record any exorcisms. Both Mark (1.23–28) and Luke (4.31–37) place Jesus delivering a demoniac as the first miracle that he performed. Exorcisms are an important part of the Markan portrait of Jesus. Four of the recorded thirteen healing miracles in his Gospel describe exorcisms.

Mark also records the relationship between exorcism and preaching – 'And he went throughout Galilee, proclaiming the message in their synagogues and casting out demons' (Mark 1.39). Luke recounts that Jesus sent his disciples out to do the same, to preach and to heal and cast out demons (Luke 9.1–6; 10.17–18).

A charismatic preacher like Wimber can claim: 'Like Jesus himself, we have a job to do: *proclaim* the kingdom of God and *demonstrate* it through healing the sick and casting out demons.'[50] For some preachers Satan and deliverance from demonic oppression or possession feature prominently in preaching a theology which depicts the kingdom of God and the realm of Satan permanently at war with each other. Satan can also be blamed if the charismatic message fails, as in the case of David Watson, the noted evangelist who died of cancer. At a major healing conference not long after his death a speaker is alleged to have remarked that 'Satan had murdered him'.[51]

For preachers like Wimber Satan is viewed as a personal devil who causes much sickness, citing such passages as Matthew 17.14–21 that speak of the demon of epilepsy. Wimber states: 'Scripture makes a distinction between natural and demonic causes of physical and mental illness. In some instances the sick were described as being "demonised", and in others they were simply called "sick". In seventeen instances in the gospels and Acts this distinction is made.'[52]

There is a readiness for some preachers to take the Gospel healing narratives as they stand and to accept uncritically all that they seem to say about the link between evil spirits and sickness. On the other hand

there are those who tend to dismiss the demonic elements in these healing stories as being a product of a
world view which no longer has a place in modern
society. Black remarks: 'We preach the "demon possession" texts and attempt to apply biblical notions of
demons to persons and issues today. Many of us inten-
tionally or unintentionally apply first-century under-
standings of the nature of illness to a postmodern
congregation because of the "authority" of the biblical
text.'[53]

Belief in the existence of evil spirits was widespread in
Jesus' day, but do we have to preach belief in demon possession just because Jesus did? How far was Jesus' attitude
sociologically determined as part of his Jewish culture? Do
we have to share a first-century world view of a developed
demonology when we preach these texts, or of a cosmic
warfare between two opposed kingdoms which lies
behind Jesus' own proclamation of the kingdom of God?
This is, of course, ultimately a Christological question
concerning whether Jesus' knowledge was limited and
conditioned by the first-century beliefs of his time. There is
also the hermeneutical question as to whether we interpret
scripture as *asserting* demonology or simply *assuming* it.

Evil spirits figure prominently in the healing narratives in the Gospels. Some preachers feel happy to use
this biblical model, language and imagery because the
spiritual battle against forces of evil appears very real
indeed. Others, however, trace evil ultimately to natural
causes and believe that where symptoms had previously
been attributed to evil spirits, now they can be seen as
having a psychological cause which can be treated by
psychiatry, counselling, etc. *A Time to Heal* comments:

The Church has always been challenged with the task of interpreting the gospel as it has come down to us in the Scriptures in the light of contemporary culture, and many argue we can no longer think and speak in terms of evil spirits, Satan or even spiritual evil. Others, while acknowledging that some demythologizing of the scriptural texts may be necessary, reply that the primitive symbolism points to spiritual evil as a reality which we cannot ignore, because even today such an evil can so dominate the lives of certain people that they need the Church's authority and power in Christ to liberate them.[54]

It is an important theological issue as to whether evil influences come from outside ourselves, or even from outside the society in which we live. There will always be differences of opinion on whether evil spirits actually exist as real entities, or whether they are just personifications of evil. Which stance we take will obviously be determinative for our preaching. Some will talk of individuals being oppressed by a spirit of lust, or anger, or jealousy not just metaphorically but as an objective reality. It may be that such preachers will also, for example, see homosexuals as being under demonic influence from which they need deliverance. Other preachers will emphasize not the individual but demonic forces which can affect societies and institutions – ideologies such as fascism and apartheid and other such social evils. These may be denounced heroically from the pulpit as the Church adopts a prophetic role. Of course, those who have witnessed Auschwitz may not be able to dismiss the notion of the demonic as at all implausible.

The worshipping environment

The setting for preaching about healing is important. This includes the impact that both the worshipping environment and the rhetorical style of the preacher have on the hearer. There is a variety of worship settings in which healing may be sought, ranging from a catholic sacramental setting through penance, the eucharist, laying on of hands and anointing of the sick, to a charismatic setting through gifts of healing and words of knowledge. Worship, the sacraments and the proclamation of the word of God are often intertwined in seeking healing. An atmosphere of faith is also important in healing, and worship and preaching can foster this. 'All Christian worship can bring healing through which we meet the living Christ and touch the hem of his garment.'[55]

Preaching on healing in an emotionally charged atmosphere can, of course, have a placebo effect or a re-creative effect. Percy expresses concern over the place of emotions in worship meetings such as those Wimber used to conduct. He remarks: 'It is people's feelings that are to be changed first (by worship), before their minds are changed (by teaching).'[56] 'A good song is often more memorable than a good sermon.'[57]

There is no doubt that the vocal force or presentational skills of the preacher can have an impact on the way the sermon is received by the hearer, and this is particularly important in healing. MacNutt speaks of how serenity can be a sign of trust and sureness, while loud proclaiming of a deep faith and trust in God's promises can indicate insecurity and anxiety. He comments about asking for healing: 'I cannot picture myself as a child sitting down at the dinner table and having to claim loudly to my father to send food down to my end of the table. Rather, I quietly ask him to pass the chicken.'[58]

It is interesting to read Percy's evaluation of Wimber, whom he sees as a marvellous rhetorician, even though he is often critical of the charismatic method. Percy says of Wimber:

> His use of vocal force is nearly always appropriate to the desired goal of his rhetorical output. Stories that illustrate healing, for example, move in a typical vocal pattern. Usually, the condition of the person and the sickness is articulated in a depressed, resigned, hopeless sort of way, helping to underline the helplessness of the sick person. The healing process is described tentatively, exemplifying the risk of faith involved. The result (success) is described in excited tones, with the pitch and speed of speech delivery rising all the time. The effect of the vocal force is to move the audience, from resignation to faith, and from faith to excitement and expectancy.[59]

The expectancy of the hearer is an important dimension in preaching. Sometimes the hearers need their expectations healed. 'If we think that God will work in our lives to keep us safe from all harm and give us all we desire, then at some point in our lives we are going to be disappointed.'[60] It is important that preachers do not raise false expectations. There are many examples of people being hurt at healing services by being made to feel guilty when they are not healed. Where does that leave the unhealed, particularly those people whose circumstances are unchangeable and whose conditions remain incurable?

With this in mind I once preached a sermon in which I spoke cautiously about healing. I was preaching on the report *A Time to Heal* which had just been published and concluded my sermon with this quote from the report: 'We seem to be moving towards the view that, whatever happened in the past, today God does not normally work through that which can be defined as miraculous.'[61] Knowing that this would not be what some of my hearers would want to hear, I felt the need to finish on a more positive note. I therefore told a story reported at that time in *Alpha News* of a woman healed of blindness. At the end of the service, a priest's wife who had recently bravely endured a seven-hour cancer operation, a woman of great faith, said to me: 'I kept waiting for you to say what I wanted you to say and finally you said it,' presumably referring to the Alpha story. She was obviously not impressed with the *A Time to Heal* conclusion. It was not what she wanted to hear in her situation. Preachers on healing need to be sensitive to the needs of the hearer, while remaining honest about expectations, and this preaching needs to take place in a conducive worshipping environment which fosters faith and hope in God.

Evidence for healing

When one thinks of evidence for healing, one begins perhaps by thinking of Lourdes or the claims made by charismatic preachers. Since the one hundred or more years' existence of the International Medical Bureau at Lourdes 65 cases have met the rigid criteria for the miraculous. The system of verification is that the prognosis must be permanent or terminal in the short-term, the cure be immediate without convalescence, be complete and lasting, and the prescribed treatment could not be attributed as the cause of the cure or be an aid to it. In addition the Bureau has records of several thousand healings that are beyond medical explanation, but which do not meet these criteria. Thousands of other claims of healing are registered annually. A priest remarked that he believed the skin between heaven and earth is thinner in Lourdes than elsewhere.

MacNutt, a respected preacher in the charismatic tradition, stated that 'in the past twenty years I think I can safely say that I have seen thousands of healings take place through prayer'.[62] Again, 'I would estimate that more than half the people for whom we pray for physical ailments are healed or are notably improved.'[63] He makes an important caveat, however: 'The most important thing I have learned in the past few years about praying for healing is that *usually* people are not completely healed by prayer, but they are *improved*.'[64] Perhaps we ought not to be surprised by this statement, as healing through medicine often works in this way.

Proof is, of course, a difficulty. To prove healing from cancer, for example, can take years of scans, tests and subsequent good health. For the believer, of course, often no argument is necessary and for the unbeliever no argument will ever prove sufficient. 'It is extremely difficult to prove medically that sudden and unexpected cures do not have some natural explanation at present unknown to science.'[65] *A Time to Heal* concludes that 'it is practically impossible to provide scientific evidence to prove without question the effectiveness of the Church's healing ministry'.[66]

Many question the claims made, for example, by charismatic preachers about healing. Hacker comments: 'Evidence for miracles is always difficult to assess, but it would appear that in some Charismatic circles enthusiasm does outrun the critical faculties. And this is given an additional impetus when "signs and wonders" are required to provide support and proof to the authenticity of the message.'[67] Preachers need to guard against being under this kind of pressure to deliver.

Stories of healings abound in sermons, but the too casual claims of some charismatic preachers concerning miraculous healings mean that the rhetoric often exceeds the reality. Many claimed healings may be at the level of the placebo effect. Accusations of exaggerated rhetoric and manipulation have certainly been levelled against the late John Wimber. The programme-makers of the TV documentary *Miracles* claimed to be unable to verify any of the 68 miraculous cures claimed on stage by Pastor Reinhard Bonnke at a rally in Benin. Yet this banner headline appeared not so long ago in a Nigerian newspaper: 'Bonnke raises man from death in Onitsha.' The man had been involved in a car accident and was allegedly certified dead on arrival at hospital and taken to the mortuary for embalming. Two days later his body was taken in a coffin to a church where Bonnke was preaching, where life returned. His serious injuries which brought about his death were also supposedly healed without trace. What are we to make of this? Charismatics in this country report a plentiful supply of healing miracles in African and other Third World countries, which they attribute to the greater faith of Christians there who are dependent upon God healing directly because of limited medical resources. But critics will ask: 'Is this not rather due to a lack of accurate verifiable reporting?'

Dr Peter May, a Southampton family doctor (GP), questions the claims made by some preachers involved in the healing ministry. He agrees with the criteria set up by the Medical Bureau at Lourdes, but does not believe they are applied rigorously enough. He claims he has never found any examples of Christ-like miracles of healing such as we see in the Gospels (e.g. a shrivelled hand, Lazarus in the tomb for four days). For people like May there appears to be a shortage of evidence of miraculous healing taking place of the kind we see in Jesus' ministry. Our assessment of contemporary evidence for healing will obviously affect our expectations and condition how we preach about healing to some extent.

A Time to Heal cautions: 'It is important to avoid making exaggerated claims of physical healing (in the context of cure) where there is no evidence to support this.'[68] However, Hacker states: 'Many of the criticisms of John Wimber, for example, are made not so much on the grounds that his claims were exaggerated, but that he distorted the Christian message by giving "signs and wonders" too much prominence.'[69] This danger of imbalance is a particular problem for those preachers engaged in the healing ministry.

3

Ways of preaching Gospel healing stories

The previous chapter raised a number of difficult theological issues which often need to be taken into account when preaching about healing. As we have seen there can be many different viewpoints on these issues. The most common approach for preaching about healing is, of course, to utilize the Gospel healing stories, as these are the most frequently used and widely read texts on the subject.

In this chapter, therefore, I look at ways of preaching about healing in which I critique four possible models for preaching the Gospel healing stories. These are not all mutually exclusive. There are, of course, other sources for preaching about healing outside the Gospels (e.g. see W. Brueggemann, *The Threat of Life: Sermons on Pain, Power and Weakness*, Fortress, Minneapolis, 1996, for a collection of sermons on Old Testament themes).

Literal model

A literal model will do what it says and interpret the healing texts in the Gospels literally. It is based on a firm belief in the historical truth of the miracles recorded in the Gospel healing narratives. A literal approach may simply mean that the preacher takes the texts at their face value as an historical record that Jesus physically healed people. However, it often carries with it the expectation that these healings can be repeated today, for God can heal our bodies with a power beyond the resources of medicine and the body's own natural capacity to heal itself. The Gospel healing texts are lifted directly out of their first-century context and applied to people and situations in the twenty-first century, with people being encouraged to seek physical healing today.

This model, therefore, often sees a direct line between Jesus' practice and contemporary healing. Jesus' healing ministry is a model, a paradigm for believers to emulate rather than a unique phenomenon. Jesus' healings are a prototype for the Church's healing ministry. It is claimed that Jesus anticipated a continual healing ministry in the Church after his resurrection. The Church inherits the promise of Jesus that his disciples will do greater works than he did (John 14.12).

Charismatic preachers, in particular, stress the continuity between the supernatural experiences described in the Gospels and the supernatural activity of God today. Such supernatural phenomena are approached with sympathy rather than scepticism. For preachers like MacNutt healing is an essential part of the message of salvation. He states: 'Personally, I believe that the attitude of most Christians today in regard to healing is shaped more by pagan thought than by Christianity. Most sermons on sickness and suffering reflect more the influence of Roman Stoicism than the doctrine of the church's founder.'[1] He also notes that 'some recently formed Pentecostal churches and groups, frequently the victims of an anti-intellectual bias, have preached universal healing, without complete balance but with great effect, while the established churches, proud of their intellectual tradition, have preached on the subject of healing with great caution but little power'.[2]

MacNutt observes that in the New Testament the first disciples did not go out to preach *and* to heal but to preach *by* healing. They preached the message of salvation by actually continuing the works of Jesus. He states: 'Preaching a doctrine of God's salvation without salvation actually taking place, or preaching about healing without healing taking place, is empty rhetoric. Perhaps this is why so much of today's preaching impresses people as abstract and irrelevant.'[3]

Some preachers, however, do not so closely identify preaching the biblical healing texts with demonstrations of such healings today. They are 'literal' preachers when it comes to assessing the historical credibility of the biblical accounts, but 'metaphorical' ones when it comes to applying the texts to today.

Bridging the gap between the biblical world and our own can be more difficult than literalists would care to admit when preaching the Gospel healing narratives. Black comments: 'One of the most difficult tasks biblical preachers face today is understanding the text in its own context and then deciding what application (if any) the text has for today. The times we live in are so drastically different than they were two thousand years ago in the Hellenistic world that it becomes very difficult to deal with the Gospel healing texts.'[4] She stresses how appalled we would be if somebody applied seventeenth-century medical concepts to illness today, given the considerable advancement of medical science since then. Yet, she says, 'We often unwittingly apply the medical world-view of biblical times to contemporary disability issues when we preach the healing narratives.' She concludes:

> Few preachers today would consider relating that medical worldview to contemporary diseases such as chicken pox, pneumonia, or cancer [...]. But disabilities such as deaf-ness, blindness, and paralysis are different, because they are found in the biblical texts. Many ministers preach on the Gospel healing narratives and apply a first-century medical perspective to persons who are blind, deaf, or paralyzed now. [...] We preach the 'demon possession' texts and attempt to apply biblical notions of demons to persons and issues today.[5]

Black's other dissatisfaction with a literal approach is that it focuses on the physical dimension of the person's illness and overlooks the social and community dimension, which I discuss later. In a number of the Gospel healing narratives, apart from the cure there is a new social acceptance of the person by Jesus, if not by the community as well. For example, the social effects of leprosy were that those afflicted had to stay outside the community, the blind or deaf had to beg to survive. Illness and disability today can similarly make people feel unwanted or a burden to society. A literal model fails to focus on this wider picture. The preacher, while holding out the hope of a cure, may only reinforce a person's sense of hopelessness and exclusion from the full life of the community if that person is not cured.

Liberal model

At the other end of the spectrum from the literal approach is the liberal model which is likely to be suspicious of any kind of supernatural miraculous healing, expecting God to work through normal means. 'Some preachers from this theological perspective do not believe in miracles and avoid preaching the healing texts altogether. Others try to explain the healings scientifically, and still others leave miracles in the realm of mystery and unexplained phenomena.'[6]

The idea that God intervenes directly in the physical world seems to liberals to be incompatible with what is known scientifically about the universe and so they find it difficult to call Jesus' healings miraculous. If all the relevant factors were known, his healings could probably be attributed to medical or psychological causes. *A Time to Heal* comments: 'Some argue that Scripture has to be read in the light of the age and culture in which the authors lived: in those days miracles were commonly associated with stories of great leaders and therefore we must accept that the miracles of the New Testament are, if not legendary, probably based on the scrappiest of historical fact.'[7] The liberal preacher is likely, therefore, to lay aside any supernatural healing in the text to pursue a current health-related topic or some other important aspect of the narrative.

Most liberals take a psychological approach to healing and tend to dismiss the New Testament miracles as examples of psychosomatic healings. It is, of course, true that one cannot draw a sharp line between the physical and the mental, and some physical symptoms are in fact psychosomatic. Likewise many of the symptoms attributed to demonic activity in Jesus' day are seen today as having physical or psychological causes. Liberals, whose views are driven by a belief that God does not intervene in a direct way in the physical world, will therefore use the healing texts metaphorically, or else lay aside discussion of the healing itself to pursue other issues in the text. For example, those who espouse a liberation theology will see Jesus not so much as a healer or redeemer, but as a revolutionary who over-turns the status quo of the rich in favour of the dispos-sessed and the poor.

Hacker draws attention to the two frameworks of the theological and the scientific: 'If we see God as being responsible directly for all that happens, then our first thought is likely to be: Why has he visited this particular illness on me at this particular time? If on the other hand we accept the normal scientific view that illness is caused by such things as viruses, we will ask a different set of questions: Who have I caught it off? Why did I let myself get run down? Why didn't I have that flu jab which the doctor suggested?'[8]

MacNutt is concerned that to limit God's power by speaking of him acting only through nature tends to make him seem distant and impersonal. He remarks: 'To insist that God does not heal puts Him "out there" and makes Him into an impersonal force even less involved in our lives than any compassionate human being would be.'[9]

Although the liberal is likely to distrust the idea of God's special intervention and will want to free the biblical texts from the constraints of literalism, some will want to treat these texts with deep seriousness and yet reinterpret or demythologize them. To take the demonic as an example, one could end up, as we shall see later (cf. p. 78), with a liberal interpretation which provides a metaphorical understanding of demons as nameless 'forces of evil'. This liberal interpretation is not necessarily denying the reality of the demonic and what happened, or devaluing its significance, but using more contemporary language to describe it. For some liberals, however, the suggestion that any force from outside ourselves can actually hold sway over us is a diminishment of human responsibility.

For the liberal who sees little evidence of God healing, the question is: 'Should we be preaching about divine healing at all?' Rabbi Harold Kussner in the television documentary *Miracles* had this to say: 'To tantalize the blind, the lame, the dying, the afflicted, the terminally ill; to dangle hope before parents of a severely afflicted child is an incredibly cruel thing to do – and, to do it in the name of God, to do it in the name of religion – I think that is unforgivable.'

Metaphorical/spiritual model

I have included in this model those who take a cessationist or dispensational view of the healing miracles and are therefore likely to apply a metaphorical/spiritual model to the healing texts. Dispensationalists defend a cessationist position which holds that miracles ceased after the apostolic age. God works through different dispensations or eras in history. In order to launch the Church the apostles were granted a special temporary dispensation to perform signs and wonders. Once the Christian Church was established, healings and other miracles were no longer required. The command to preach was given for all time, but the command to heal was meant to apply to the early years of the Church to help get it started. God has now withdrawn that power to heal and modern medicine fulfils the New Testament promises about healing today. There is, however, no basis for this view in the New Testament.

Many preachers today do not hold to either of the first two models I have discussed, the literal and the liberal models, when preaching healing texts, but hover somewhere between the two perspectives. 'They do not believe in the literal interpretation of the Bible and are not willing to make a commitment to faith healing and contemporary miracles, yet they also do not want to deny the possibility of miracles, the effect of sin on one's life, or the importance of faith. Their approach to the healing narratives is to preach these texts metaphorically.'[10] There are, of course, those who adopt a literal approach to the healing texts who, because they do not link them with demonstrations of such healings today, will also want to apply them metaphorically, as may be the case too with those who adopt an opposing liberal approach to the healing miracles.

A metaphorical approach will see sickness and disability as a metaphor for the state of humanity generally. Texts on blindness or deafness may be used to talk about being deaf to the word of God or blind to spiritual realities or sin. A spiritual approach may concentrate on suffering in sickness as playing an important part in spiritual growth. Suffering is seen as a mark of the Christian life after the pattern of Jesus who used the healing of disease to illustrate on a physical level what he wants to do for us spiritually.

It is certainly true that the Gospel writers, especially Mark and John, see a correlation between physical blindness or deafness and that of an attitude of spiritual hardness. So, homiletically, texts referring to these physical conditions have often been preached metaphorically, almost always with a negative or sinful connotation. The hymn *Amazing Grace* is a classic example of this with its wording 'I once was lost, but now am found, was blind, but now I see', which equates blindness with a pre-Christian state.

Black is concerned about the effect such preaching has on disabled people today, for the manner in which preachers often expound healing texts can be oppressive to people with disabilities, which alienates and excludes them. This is particularly so when disability is inadvertently linked with sin and lack of faith. She is concerned about the result of using these terms metaphorically:

The words themselves carry with them a negative connotation, and deafness, blindness, and paralysis become equated with sin. The metaphorical usage is transferred onto those who live with these physical realities on a daily basis. The negative result may be somewhat softened by those preachers who clarify their metaphorical use of these terms by preceding them with the word 'spiritual': as in 'spiritual blindness' or 'spiritual deafness.' But for those who live with these physical realities, using blindness, deafness, and paralysis metaphorically continues to contribute to the negative, oppressive attitudes people have towards persons who are blind, deaf, or paralyzed.[11]

The concern is that if we talk, for example, of blind Bartimaeus representing all of us in our spiritual blindness, this may be heard by a physically blind person as saying that blindness is a sign of sin in that person. If the preacher then goes on to say that we need to change our spiritual attitude or resistance to God so that we may see again, what does that imply to a blind person whose physical condition also needs changing, but for whom change is not a matter of personal choice? Black concludes:

> Persons with disabilities then, carry the double burden of those who preach these Gospel healing narratives from the perspective that if only their faith were strong enough, they would be cured, which implies that disability is a punishment for sin or for lack of faith; and those who preach these texts metaphorically, using blindness, deafness, and paralysis as analogies of sin. Either way, the liberating word of 'healing' is fundamentally missing for persons with disabilities.[12]

Social/community model

A final model for preaching the healing stories in the Gospels is the social/community approach. This focuses on the reintegration back into society of the sick and disabled who had previously been marginalized as a result of their condition. In recent homiletical literature on healing one of the key texts is that by Kathy Black, who particularly espouses a social/community model for preaching Gospel healing stories. That is why reference is made to her *A Healing Homiletic* on a number of occasions. She points to the miracle of social transformation started by Jesus and advocates a way of preaching the healing texts as good news which shows Jesus' acceptance of people with disabilities. This contrasts with the culture and attitude of his day which socially marginalized the disabled. The community is therefore called to imitate Jesus' example of acceptance.

The synoptic writers stress the importance of community and how Jesus' healing ministry is compassionately directed to people on the very edge of society – the dispossessed, the marginalized and the social outcast. For example, lepers were excluded from society without any real hope of returning to the community. Jesus healing the leper (Matthew 8.2–4; Mark 1.40–45; Luke 5.12–16) allowed the leper's reintegration back into society. Jesus' healings had social effects which saw barriers which separated people come down, social wholeness restored and people return to their family and friends.

In the case of the healing of the woman with a haemorrhage (Matthew 9.20–22; Mark 5.25–34; Luke 8.43–48), her physical condition made her socially and ceremonially unclean and in danger of defiling those with whom she came into contact. This produced serious social and emotional problems for her. Indeed, her social predicament would have been as distressing as her physical illness. Her healing, therefore, involved not only her physical well-being but also her social reinvolvement in the life of the community.

Many disabled people today are not requesting healing, but are merely asking to be accepted as they are. One of the problems of some charismatic preachers is that their theology can imply that the permanently disabled are unacceptable as they are, both to God and to society. 'Some people in the disability community feel it would have been better if Jesus had healed the *community* of its common practice of ostracizing all those with disabilities, rather than performing miraculous cures on the persons with disabilities themselves.'[13] Often society needs to be healed of its intolerance, for communities contribute massively to a person's sense of well-being whether in the workplace, family, school, club or whatever. With this social/community model the Gospel healing stories can be preached as good news by focusing on those elements in them which show Jesus' acceptance of people with disabilities, in contrast to the general attitude of his day.

Adopting a social/community model for preaching about healing may not just be about the healing of individuals like the leper, coupled with their reintegration back into society and society's acceptance of them. It may also involve addressing the fact that society itself is also sick in various ways and God's healing word and power need to be brought to bear on the still wider causes of ill health – social, economic, environmental, etc. For example, liberation theology preaches the possibility of change. Healing depends as much on altering people's contexts and the social causes of illness as anything else.

Preaching the healing word has to be set in the context of the local community. What are the local issues and social evils that need healing? – social decay, vandalism, unemployment, crime, etc. What are the deep-rooted sicknesses in our local and national life? 'The God who heals is also a God who looks for the righting of wrongs, and if the way to a healthier world involves combating poverty, injustice, violence, the exploitation of the environment, and other evils, then that is something which also has to be accepted, and indeed welcomed, as part of what it means to engage in a "ministry of healing".'[14]

These are some of the issues which need addressing from our pulpits, above all to be backed up by social action if we are to see 'creation healed', as Hans Küng defines salvation. We are indeed to 'go and preach the gospel, using words if necessary.' MacNutt sums it up beautifully: 'The alcoholic was given sermons and told to repent. Some were helped. But it took Alcoholics Anonymous to show that a community of support was needed for most alcoholics to make a comeback.'[15]

The four models that I have described above are not all mutually exclusive, of course. One's expectations, or lack of them, concerning healing will obviously influence which model preachers adopt and the way in which they preach as well as minister to the sick.

4

Preaching controversial issues

I examine in this chapter the application of the models or ways of preaching about healing, set out in the previous chapter, to two of the key issues identified in Chapter 2. I have taken the issues 'Sickness as a punishment for sin' and 'Healing and the demonic' to exemplify the different modes of preaching about healing, as these tend to be somewhat controversial.

Sickness as a punishment for sin

The key texts are Mark 2.1–12; John 5.1–15ff. and John 9.1–3ff. In two of these narratives – the healing of the paralytic (Mark 2) and the healing of the man at the pool of Beth-zatha (John 5) – Jesus appears to acknowledge the interrelationship between sickness and sin and to heal by proclaiming the forgiveness of sins. In the healing of the blind man in John 9, however, Jesus went against the popular belief of his day that sickness and sin were related. He denied that there was a direct link between the man's blindness and his sins or those of his parents. Homileticians and commentators vary in the way they approach these texts. Many preachers focus on Mark 2 and John 5 and the supposed relationship between sickness and sin, while others play down such a link by focusing on John 9. Let us, then, apply the four preaching models to this issue with examples from various sermons.

Literal model

The Mark 2 text is often used as a justification for the theology that sin is the cause of sickness. Preachers like Wimber and MacNutt recount in sermons stories of people with physical ailments who see their conditions disappear when they repent of their sins. Some fundamentalist preachers see a close connection between sin and sickness in drug abuse, HIV/AIDS, sexual promiscuity, etc. They see AIDS as a judgement of God. James Anderton, the former Chief Constable of Manchester, dubbed 'God's cop' by the press, was much criticized for speaking at a seminar on AIDS in 1986 of homosexuals, prostitutes and drug addicts 'swirling in a cesspit of their own making'.[1]

There is, however, a balanced way of preaching a literal model, as I tried to do in a sermon I preached at St Marylebone on Mark 2.1–12, of which here is an extract:

> Now let's look more closely at this story of Jesus healing the paralytic. There is a link in this story as we have it handed down to us between sickness and sin, which I want to take a look at – because I sometimes come across people who feel that their sickness is a result of their sin. They feel that God is afflicting them in some way, that's why they're sick. This is what subconsciously sometimes lies behind a person's cry, 'Why is this happening to me? What have I *done* to deserve this?' Is there a link between our sin and

our sickness? Well, at first sight in this story that seems to be the case.

After retelling the story in narrative style in an imaginative way I continued:

> The Jews in Palestine in Jesus' day connected sin and suffering in a way that we don't today. They argued that if a man was suffering he must have sinned. The Rabbis had a saying: 'There is no sick man healed of his sickness until all his sins have been forgiven.' There appears to be a connection between sin and sickness in the healing of an invalid in John 5 when Jesus said to him, 'Sin no more so that nothing worse happens to you.' [...] To the Jews of Jesus' day a sick person was someone with whom God was angry. Now what are we to make of that? Well, it is true that *some* illnesses *are* due to sin. Some people's health *has* been broken as a direct result and consequence of their sinful behaviour (we read about it all the time). It is even more true that individual people suffer because of the sins of others (we see it in the persecutions in East Timor and other places and in terrorist acts of violence). *Sometimes* there *is* a connection between sin and sickness or suffering. We also know today that some illnesses are psychosomatic. A sick mind produces a sick body. So a sinful guilt-ridden disposition *can* result in an unhealthy body, and therefore inner harmony and wholeness or holiness need to be restored before physical healing can take place. Forgiveness needs to be experienced first. So maybe this paralysis in this man *was* a direct result of his sin and Jesus saw this and that is why he said, 'Son, your sins are forgiven' before he could say, 'Rise, take up your stretcher and walk.'

I then gave a contemporary illustration of this before proceeding:

Sometimes sin and sickness *are* linked, as appears to be the case in the Gospel story today. We may be afflicted because of our sin. *But* it is more normally true that sickness and suffering are *not*, I repeat *not*, a punishment for sin. That suffering is a punishment from God is a doctrine of Hinduism – the doctrine of Karma. This was what some of the row was about when Glenn Hoddle was removed as the England football manager – his alleged views about reincarnation and disability. The reason why people are in a wheelchair now is because of sins they committed in a former life. It's their fault that they cannot walk. It's a punishment for their sins.

In John's Gospel, however, when the disciples came to Jesus about the man who was blind from his birth and said to him, 'Rabbi, who sinned, this man or his parents that he had been born blind?' Jesus replied, 'Neither this man sinned nor his parents that he was born blind.' That's not the explanation of suffering in this case – that it's a punishment from God. It's not! So our conclusion is that *sometimes* sickness and suffering *are* brought about by sin, as appears to be the case in the Gospel today. Normally, however, sickness and suffering are *not*, of course, to be seen as God afflicting us in some way. [...]

I think this is a balanced way of preaching a link between sickness and sin using a literal model which is faithful to the texts but does not dogmatize on the relationship between the two.

Liberal model
The liberals' starting point for preaching on this issue is the question of how God acts in relation to his universe. They do not see God intervening directly in it and thereby visiting illness upon people. Liberal preachers

may, therefore, concentrate on criticizing a literalist approach to this issue, or go on to find other alternative ways of preaching these texts.

A critical approach could utilize the Mark 2 text and point out that many scholars believe that the controversy over the forgiveness of sins is a later addition to an earlier healing story which originally stood on its own. Verse 10 of this narrative 'implies that the healing of the man with paralysis was proof that Jesus had authority on earth to forgive sins. Since healing did not imply power to forgive sins, and given the situation of the early church, it is likely that verse 10 was not said by the earthly Jesus, but was added to the story by the early Christian church.'[2] However, Jesus' response is 'not in itself sufficient reason for supposing that two stories have been joined together. Certainly for Mark, healing and forgiveness belong together.'[3] If Mark 2.5b–10 is a later addition this would support a liberal interpretation and throw doubt on the validity of the claims of those who preach this text as justifying a theology that links sin with sickness.

Again, a more liberal approach may stress that the importance of the narrative in Mark 2.1–12 is not the healing but the person of Jesus. The real issue for the author, it may be claimed, is not Jesus' healing of the paralytic but the person of Jesus, who he was and his claims to be equal with God. It may therefore focus on this aspect.

In the John 5 text a liberal model may draw attention to the uncertainties in the story. In my own preaching of this text using a literal model in a sermon at St Marylebone I switched for a time towards a liberal model, following the retelling of the story, by saying:

That's the end of the story as far as the author is concerned. – *It's not as far as I'm concerned!* There are still some outstanding questions I want answers to. Quite apart from why did God allow this man to suffer for 38 years, I want to know why Jesus apparently healed just one sick man in Beth-zatha, when there was a multitude of sick people there? What about the rest? What about the plight of those who are not cured today when they seek the healing Christ? Why is there no reference to anyone having any faith in this story? Is there really a link between this man's sickness and his sin when Jesus tells him to sin no more so that nothing worse happens to him? What about the apparently stupid question Jesus asked a man who had been ill for 38 years: 'Do you want to be made well?'

A liberal model may, of course, not only go on to ask further such questions but also question the whole basis of the miraculous nature of the story in John 5.

Liberals may focus on John 9 and discuss how some people blame the parents for the suffering that their children experience in life, but point out that this is not the same as believing that God is punishing the children because of the irresponsibility of the parents. The liberal may also want to shift the focus to how human sinfulness contributes to sickness and ill health in the world, pointing out that one of the biggest causes of suffering worldwide is poverty and how there is a direct link between sickness and human greed – it is, however, in this case the guilty who escape punishment and the innocent who suffer.

Other preachers utilizing this model may try to psychologize the issue of sin and sickness. As Hacker describes it: 'It has now been clearly established that there can be a link between negative feelings and the immune system, so that helping someone to overcome their feelings of guilt or bitterness is not just a matter of making them "feel better". It may have important consequences for their actual physical health.'[4] Hooker in her commentary on Mark's Gospel, quoting a psychiatrist friend, speaks of the likelihood that a sense of guilt *could* cause paralysis and that the assurance of forgiveness *could* bring about a cure.

Liberal preachers do not then generally expect God to heal sickness supernaturally through the miraculous. They will be even less inclined to see illness being sent by God as an affliction to punish sin. They are likely, therefore, to avoid preaching the healing aspects of the texts altogether in Mark 2 and John 5 or focus positively instead on some other aspect of the texts or on a health-related issue. Otherwise they may preach negatively using John 9 by criticizing the literalist position, often with an anti-charismatic polemic – Jesus did not link sickness/disability with sin in this passage and it would be unwise for us to do so, they will argue.

A liberal approach may, of course, just seek to illustrate the distress such a link between sin and suffering can bring to sick people, particularly the agonizing of soul if they make the link themselves rather than having it made for them. Perhaps one of the saddest pastoral moments for me was when I visited a very eminent retired senior hospital consultant who had Parkinson's Disease. He remarked to me: 'I'm afraid, Christopher, God is not on my side. God is not pleased with me and that is why I'm being afflicted.' I was saddened that such an eminent doctor should attribute his Parkinson's

Disease to punishment by God. Is it not rather that he is now eighty-six?

Metaphorical/spiritual model

This model sees sickness as a metaphor for the state of humanity generally. Suffering may be seen as playing an important part in spiritual growth and Jesus' healings as illustrating physically what he wants to do for us spiritually. In John 9 and other blindness texts we have already seen the problem of speaking metaphorically about blindness in relation to an attitude of spiritual hardness or of equating blindness with a pre-Christian state. This way of preaching can be oppressive to people with disabilities such as blindness.

An interesting example of preaching this model can be seen in Rico Tice's sermon on John 5 preached at All Souls, Langham Place entitled *Jesus meets a paralytic.*[5] His approach to this story is to spiritualize it and make metaphorical connections. The following is an extract from it which interprets Jesus' question 'Do you want to be healed?' as 'Do you want to change?':

> The sick man thought, 'Well, there's no way I can change.' And it would have been easy, wouldn't it, for the physical weakness and mental depression and a sense of helpless despair just to take over his life and to remove from him any real desire or hope or expectation that things could ever be different, that they could ever change. Do you have that feeling in some areas of your life, that actually 'No, that area will never change. I've just got to live with it. I'm in despair. That relationship will never change. That job will never change.'? Whatever it is. And that is the essence of weakness, whether it's spiritual or physical weakness.

The essence of it is that we feel that there is no way there can be any change. We feel locked in. There's no possibility to change the situation. We are just victims. We're helpless. We can't help ourselves. Physically that was the case with this man. Spiritually it may well be the case for you – it's certainly for me in one or two areas. We are unable to help ourselves. We just think 'Well, I've had it in this area.' And the parallel between spiritual weakness that every human being suffers and this one is pretty exact, I think. For, just as this man was physically so weak and had to be asked, 'Do you want to change?', so spiritually we need to be asked sometimes, 'Do you want to change?'; and just as some people wallow in their physical weakness, there are many who wallow in their spiritual weakness: 'Oh, I'm hopeless, I'm hopeless, I can't do it. Oh Rico, I wish I had your faith.'

This man had this physical weakness. What about us? Do we have that sort of spiritual experience? We feel this spiritual weakness [...]. Let's take the question Jesus asks here seriously: Do you really want to be the kind of Christian that God intended you to be? Do you really want to be the person he created you to be? Do you really want to be well? Or are you unwilling to repent, unwilling to believe? [...] Christ can change from the inside out – we know that. He can give us strength over temptation and sin. He can give us new direction and purpose. He can give us the deep love for others. But do we want him to do that? Do we want him to change us? So let's be personal. What is the spiritual issue with you that's actually been there maybe a long time and actually you don't want Christ to change it?

We can see from Rico Tice's approach that we have moved from the physical to the spiritual and have sidestepped the bodily healing miracle in order to pursue a metaphorical interpretation. The possibility of a link between this man's sickness and his sin has facilitated this kind of progression, although even this is not dwelt on in favour of an even more spiritualized approach. It is interesting to see where Tice finishes up:

> Christ gives his word of command and with it the strength and power to obey. There was no struggle for this man, just a healing word from Jesus. [...] A miracle happened. Here is God's strength in weakness and the key here – and actually the key to this whole talk is this – that the vehicle of strength is the word of Jesus. Let me say that again: the vehicle of change, the vehicle of strength for this man, were the words of Jesus. And that is the significant thing. There's no strength in religion, in this building, there's no strength here, there's no strength in outward forms of religion. No, the source of strength is Jesus Christ alone. And as he says to this man, 'Rise, pick up your mat and walk,' he says to us too: 'Turn from your sin, believe, get up and start again and trust me to give you the power to change. Experience my strength in the place of your weakness.' [...] You know when you first wake up in the morning you have a choice: am I going to get up and read the word of God and pray or am I going to lie here for another twenty minutes? Do you have that experience? [...] This is the battle every morning as I wake. 'God, now please help me to obey.' And as I do that he provides the strength. But the new life begins as I obey Jesus' powerful words. [...] So let's commit ourselves to walk in the strength that he supplies, that his words give, so that we may change.

Here then is the classic metaphorical approach with its emphasis on the spiritual principles and implications arising from a physical healing miracle, rather than concentrating on the healing itself or on the possibility of this physical manifestation being replicated again today.

Social/community model

The focus of this model lies beyond the healing miracles in the reintegration back into society of the paralytic in Mark 2 and his counterpart in John 5 and of the man born blind in John 9. All of these had been socially marginalized as a result of their disabilities by the attitude and culture of their day. Black points to the miracle of transformation started by Jesus and advocates a way of preaching these healing texts as good news which shows Jesus' acceptance of people with disabilities, which the Christian community is called to imitate.

This preaching model will move on from the healing of the individual to the healing of the community and its practice of marginalizing those with disabilities, to show how the disabled can become an integral part of the community. Such preaching will seek to change the personal and social attitudes and structures and negative attitudes of society. These people in the healing texts were not only able to walk or see again, but they were also rid of the stigma that held that these conditions were *their* fault.

Sermons on these texts will not only advocate acceptance and integration of the marginalized into society but will also attack 'the underlying economic, racial, and gendered structures of oppression which still exist and are often not dealt with. Addressing physical symptoms of alienation without also addressing the structural and attitudinal forms of alienation that are the root causes does not bring true healing to people's lives.'[6] This means that a sermon utilizing this model will focus on the sins *against* a person that results in sickness and suffering, rather than the sins committed *by* a person. It will focus, Black urges, on ways in which people who have been ostracized because of age, disability, sexual orientation, gender, ethnicity or belief can be brought from the margins into the healing presence of Christ.

Another possible way of preaching the Mark 2 text, which Black advocates, is to focus on the people carrying the paralytic, who could not get through the front door of the house and so they lowered him through the roof. Their determination and ingenuity found an unconventional alternative access through which to bring the paralytic, alienated by attitude and architecture, into the healing presence of Christ. How important disabled access is to allow entry to be gained by those with disabilities into the meeting place of the faith community.

My own sermon on Mark 2 draws attention to the social and community implications of this narrative when bringing in the faith element of this story:

> I want you to notice in this story, however, that it is *not* the faith of the paralytic that Jesus observed. 'Seeing *their* faith' probably refers to the faith of the four men who lifted him up on a stretcher and laid him at the feet of Jesus. We're not told whether the paralytic himself had any faith. [...] You see, when someone is sick or suffering, or depressed and downcast, or sinful and guilt-ridden, they often don't have *any* faith, or if they do it's at a very low ebb. Therefore, it's important that others are exercising faith on that person's behalf, that friends and loved ones are praying for them and that they are taking *active*

steps to aid their recovery. You and I are called to be stretcher bearers, to bear one another's burdens and to lift people into the healing presence of Christ through our prayers and our actions. We must look for those opportunities. We also hope that one day when *we* are on *our* sick beds, as all of us will have occasion to be, others will lift *us* up in this way.

In my introductory chapter I quoted from the *Church Times* review of the television programme *Miracles* about Lourdes, how 'millions come to experience the real miracle of finding meaning, by experiencing love which is both human and divine, in suffering and death'. Another way of drawing out the social/community implications of a passage like John 5 is to focus on the pool of Beth-zatha as a healing shrine at which the sick gathered to make pilgrimage, as at Lourdes. People want to come together to a spiritual place of prayer and penance, hope and comfort, even if they are not healed. As a wife of a dying husband said, 'Our trip to Lourdes was the fulfilment of his life and it was there that he came to terms with death. That was the miracle.' Another woman came with her handicapped child. 'I was so angry and bitter,' she said, 'but after being here amongst so much suffering I accepted it. It was a huge relief.' The presence of thousands of sick and disabled people means that they are more likely to be touched by meeting vulnerable humanity than by the supernatural. As the priest who instigated the Westminster Diocesan Pilgrimage to Lourdes said: 'Miracles happen in the smallest of ways. People learn to laugh again, or they let go. By the end of the week they are fused in a common bond of love, peace and acceptance.'[7]

These are some of the social/community implications that could find their way into sermons on healing. When one sees at Lourdes the number of people having their confessions heard before going down into the water with the hope of healing, one is reminded again of the link between sickness and sin in the story of the man lying by the side of the pool of Beth-zatha.

Healing and the demonic

There are six incidents in the Gospels, recounted in 14 texts, that refer to people who have a demon or unclean spirit within them. They are:

1   The man in the synagogue with an unclean demon (Mark 1.23–28; Luke 4.31–37)
2   The blind and dumb demoniac (Mark 3.22–27; Matthew 12.22–32; Luke 11.14–23)
3   The Gadarene demoniac(s) who lived among the tombs (Mark 5.1–20; Matthew 8.28–34; Luke 8.26–39)
4   The daughter of the Syrophoenician/Canaanite woman (Mark 7.24–30; Matthew 15.21–28)
5   The boy with convulsions/demon of epilepsy (Mark 9.14–29; Matthew 17.14–21; Luke 9.37–43)
6   The restoration of the dumb demoniac (Matthew 9.32–34)

There are also some summary statements of Jesus' healing referring to demon possession, e.g. Mark 1.32; Matthew 4.24. The Gospel writers included these various texts to show Jesus' power over evil. These exorcisms are signs of the coming of the messianic age, for the reign of God is being established by the overthrow of Satan.

As with the previous issue, preachers and commentators vary in the way they approach this area. Many today would equate so-called demonic behaviour with mental illness or some kind of addiction. Some preachers, however, still focus on demons that require exorcizing, on people who need some kind of deliverance ministry, because demons are seen to be the cause of the affliction. Let us, then, apply the four preaching models to this issue with various examples.

Literal model

Charismatic preachers like Reinhard Bonnke and the late John Wimber frequently describe exorcisms and demon possession or oppression in their preaching, particularly at evangelistic rallies or healing conferences. Wimber states: 'Many people experience chronic problems – spiritual, psychological, physical – from which they never find true healing through medicine, psychology, psychiatry or prayer. I believe that often demons are the cause of these problems.'[8] His preaching draws attention to how scripture describes areas of our lives which may be affected by demonization – dumbness, blindness, epilepsy, crippling, etc. His demonology is highly imaginative. For example, at a healing seminar in 1981 he preached: 'There are many demons that don't have a body. Having a body [for a demon] is like having a car. They want to have a car so they can get around. If they don't have a body, they're a second-class demon.

They're not first-class. I'm not kidding you. That's the way it works. And so [to them] having a body is a big deal. That's why they won't want to give it up.'[9]

Satan, demons, the spirit world, deliverance from demonic possession or oppression can all play a significant part in charismatic preaching and ministry. Satan is seen to oppose God's power and spread sin and sickness. MacNutt describes deliverance ministry as such: 'I have seen unusual phenomena take place which I think can best be explained by demonic activity. Such phenomena would include being thrown to the ground, and what purport to be demons speaking through the person (saying, for example, "You will never drive us out; we are too many and too strong for you").'[10] He describes how demons seem to have identities and names: 'The person asking for prayer knows who the demon is or what its characteristic activity is. For instance, *if* sexual sins in a given instance should happen to be demonic in causation, then the prayer can be directed against a spirit of lust. This is not to say that all sexual problems are demonic.'[11] He talks elsewhere of demons seeming to go in clusters so that a spirit of 'anger' may be attached to a spirit of 'resentment' or 'jealousy', etc. Preachers in this mould, therefore, still focus on demons and the need for exorcisms.

Black expresses considerable concern with regard to this preaching model: 'What is of concern is how we preach the texts that deal with demon possession. When a person has a form of epilepsy that cannot be totally controlled by medication or when someone has a mental illness, and we preach these texts by implying that such people are also possessed by demons, we add a tremendous burden to their already difficult lives.'[12] She is concerned over the damage such preaching can do to a person's faith:

> What damage do we do to people's faith when we implicitly or explicitly proclaim that they are possessed by a demon? [...] What barriers do we erect between them and God? When they need the love and support of God, we tell them they are in league with the devil and imply that it is their fault. [...] When demon possession is equated with evil and epilepsy and mental illness are identified as demon possession in the Synoptics, then the message is conveyed that mental illness and epilepsy are evil.[13]

Liberal model

Newbigin describes modern thinking about the demonic in the Bible as follows:

> We must look at what the Gospels have to say about hostile spiritual powers, about Satan, and about what the Fourth Gospel calls 'the ruler of this world'. If I am not mistaken, most scholarly readers of the New Testament in the past 150 years have regarded all this language as something which we can for practical purposes ignore, because it belongs to a thought world which we have grown out of.[14]

Indeed, liberals often see all this imagery about angels and demons as no different from those who used to believe in elves and fairies. Modern liberal preachers, therefore, try to reinterpret such concepts. For example, Fuller, in commenting on the exorcism in Luke 11, draws attention to why the early Church selected this passage as the Gospel to be preached on the Third Sunday of Lent. The catechumens were being instructed in preparation for baptism at Easter when they too would be exorcized, for they were transferring from the realm of Satan to the kingdom of God. He goes on to say from a liberal perspective:

> We too are now being exorcised, and we too are warned of the dangers that face us. Of course, we no longer believe in demons: 'It is impossible to use electric lights and the wireless and to avail ourselves of modern medical and surgical discoveries, and at the same time to believe in the New Testament world of spirits and miracles' (R. Bultmann). But we are bound to believe in what the demons of the New Testament signify. We need not *eliminate* the devil from the catechism but must *interpret* what he stands for. He stands for the supra-personal reality of evil, something outside ourselves which gets us in its grip. The old mythology may still be used, but it must be understood as a symbolic expression of the realities of human experience.[15]

This is the kind of reinterpretative exercise that will be undertaken by liberal preachers who seek to demythologize what they see as the primitive symbolism of the scriptural texts and emphasize human responsibility and freedom. In so doing a liberal model may seek to criticize literalist preaching along the lines we have already noted, not least because of its practical implications. 'No matter what one believes about demon possession [...] epilepsy should not be preached so as to imply that persons with epilepsy or mental illness today are possessed by demons. Persons who experience these illnesses, as well as their families and loved ones, suffer enough from social stigmas without the additional undue burden of being told they are possessed by demons.'[16]

Literalists will point out, however, that although the Gospel writers were medically ignorant (apart from

Luke to some extent) they did not put all illness down to demonic activity. They distinguished between healing and casting out demons (e.g. Luke 4.40f.; 9.1f.; 13.32) – demons are expelled, diseases are healed. But they do see suffering as one of the ways in which Satan binds mankind. Green resists the liberals' dismissal of Satan and the demonic in these strong terms:

> As we observe the variety of forms in which evil, no less than good, shows itself, are we not to suppose that there is an organising spirit of supreme evil and malignity? The name we give to it is Satan. [...] Do we not see in every generation men who seem to be the very embodiment of evil – monsters in their time? It is very hard to believe of them that wickedness is merely the absence of good. [...] I would like to ask theologians who are sceptical about the devil how they can give a satisfactory account of God if Satan is a figment of the imagination. Without the devil's existence, the doctrine of God, a God who could have made such a world and allowed such horrors as take place daily within it, is utterly monstrous. Such a God would be no loving Father. He would be a pitiless tyrant.[17]

Metaphorical/spiritual model

The term 'demon' is sometimes used as a metaphor today. Those who have an alcohol or drug addiction, those with certain kinds of mental illness, and those who feel their lives to be out of control may describe the experience as having a 'demon' within. The metaphor deals with the feeling that something else has taken over one's life and will. But this is metaphorical usage and is not meant literally. It does not indicate a belief that an evil spirit has actually taken up habitation in the body.[18]

Utilizing this model preachers may draw out certain spiritual principles from the text which emphasize Jesus, not just as a great teacher, but as the one who appears in the Gospels as the triumphant conqueror over the source of evil. Hence Beasley-Murray comments:

> From this point of view one can see why such a circumstantial narrative as that of the Epileptic Boy was preserved by Mark (9.14ff.): the pitiable condition of the child, the helplessness of the disciples and Jewish teachers alike, the agony out of which the confession of faith was wrung from the father, and the power of Christ to heal by a word, all present a unique parallel to the deliverance which He performs for every believer. There is no reason why we moderns should hesitate to use such a story today, for the sufferings of the lad are characteristic of the agonies of multitudes of our age. Despite all the endeavours of men there is still only one Deliverer. His triumphs continue to bear witness to His power to rescue the most needy of men.[19]

This metaphorical approach, which deals with the overarching spiritual principle of being rescued and delivered from the power of evil, can therefore avoid being too precise about the nature of the demonic.

Another way of using this model in preaching this issue is to focus on another aspect of the narrative rather than the demonic itself. An example of this can be seen in the following extract from a sermon preached by Paul Williams at All Souls, Langham Place on Matthew 8.28–34,[20] which deals with a spiritual principle relating to the text. It is the principle of getting our priorities right:

The demons came out and went into the pigs and the whole herd rushed down the steep bank into the lake and died in the water. [...] That's the point that everyone gets hung up over. Lead a Bible study on this passage and there's one dominant reaction. Know what it is? – 'Poor pigs!' Everybody says it. Why did Jesus do that to the pigs? [...] It's always the issue though, isn't it. Poor pigs! That's how the people of the town reacted. They wanted Jesus to leave (verse 34 quote).

You see, this story reveals priorities. The people of the town were so upset about the pigs they asked Jesus to leave (verse 33 quote). It was those tending the pigs who ran down to the town and reported all this about the pigs and *then* they included what happened to the demon-possessed men. Very interesting that order, isn't it? What happened to the demon-possessed men was not the first thing the pig herders spoke about. [...] Breathlessly they reported, 'Our pigs are dead, they've rushed over the cliff like lemmings. We're ruined. Our livelihood is gone! It's that man Jesus Christ. He exorcized those two madmen who live up by the tombs.' – It's obvious what they're upset about, isn't it? Their pigs had died. Their livelihoods were ruined. It's obvious the people of the town weren't concerned for the two men. For if they had been, rather than plead that Jesus left their region as they do in verse 34, they'd have pleaded with him to stay.

Now we've heard how those tending the pigs would have reported the incident. The two men would have told the story quite differently, wouldn't they? – 'Our lives have been transformed. Now we *have* a life. We can return to the village. We can enjoy life with our families. We've got so much to thank Jesus for.' [...] So you see who had the right priorities here? The people of the town were more bothered about the pigs than the demon-possessed men. Their priority was for themselves, for their livelihoods. And you see, our reaction to this incident will declare our hand as well. Our reaction shows who we're most bothered about – the pigs or the people. Who we most prefer, the swine or the Saviour. When this passage was read did you rejoice that Jesus had delivered these men or were you hung up over the pigs?

Another approach that could be taken to the demonic in utilizing this model is the socio-psychological approach. For example, in Luke's version of this story concerning the legion of demons (Luke 8.26–39), metaphorical connections could be made between mental illness and military or political oppression. 'This narrative may be one that tells the story of a community that is politically and economically oppressed, a community that feels it is controlled by demonic foreign powers over which it has no control.'[21] The 'legion' of demons is, in this case, metaphorically the Roman military power and the drowning of the demons represents the aspiration of political liberation from Roman occupation. This kind of metaphorical interpretation has social/community implications which we now move on to consider.

Social/community model

This model focuses on the individual sufferer in the context of their local community, or else on the demonic in relation to the wider context of societies and nations. With regard to the former Black asks the question 'What would be a healing touch, a message of hope for people who have some association with mental illness who are sitting in the pew?' She focuses on the compassion of Jesus to those who are alienated, homeless and in the depths of despair. He offers them respect and a sense of belonging by helping them to regain control of their lives and returning them to their homes, relationships and rightful places in the community.

In the story of the demoniac in Luke 8 Black draws attention to certain features of the story for preaching purposes which reinforce the community setting. The first is where Jesus sends him away saying, 'Return to your home and declare how much Jesus has done for you' (v. 39). She sees this entrusting of the man with responsibility as a gesture of respect by Jesus which brought purpose and meaning to the man's life. She states: 'He was able to contribute something back into the community, to be an interdependent part of the whole rather than being totally dependent upon others. That is an important part of the healing process for those with severe mental illnesses. It should be taken slowly, but trusting them with responsibility and giving them meaning in life as an interdependent part of the community is very important.'[22]

The supportive healing community of the Church has much to offer people living with mental illness or those who are battling with the many psychological 'demons' that can grip people. That is why at St Marylebone we have a healing and counselling centre staffed by trained counsellors and psychotherapists.

Black also draws attention to another aspect of the Luke 8 text where, following the healing of the man, the people 'were seized with great fear' (v. 37). She states:

> For healing and full participation to happen, the church and society must deal with their own feelings of being 'seized with fear' when in the presence of something they

do not understand. Fear is the greatest barrier to healing –
both for those who need the healing and for those who
offer a helping hand. It is fear that causes the townsfolk in
the text to act irrationally and send Jesus away. [...] We
need to address our irrational fears before we can be a
healing presence in the lives of those who live with mental
illness.[23]

This is one way of preaching about healing and the
demonic using this social/community model, which
focuses on the individual sufferer in the context of his/
her local community.

However, another way of tackling this model would be
to deal with the demonic on a larger scale, in relation to
the wider context of societies and nations. 'The idea that
the gospel is addressed only to the individual and that it is
only indirectly addressed to societies, nations, and cultures
is simply an illusion of our individualistic post-
Enlightenment Western culture.'[24] Newbigin is concerned
about the demonic in social and political structures, particularly the 'demonic power of *apartheid*'[25] and how no
one in South Africa doubted its reality and power. He
acknowledges that while there has to be some kind of
ordered structure of power in institutions and society, this
can be either benevolent or malevolent. We have to
acknowledge their reality and power and ask what the
gospel has to do with them, he says. He states: 'There has
to be some kind of ordered structure of power. Without it,
human life would dissolve into anarchy. These structural
elements are necessary to guide and protect human life.
They serve God's purpose. But, as we well know, they can
also become demonic. The God-given authority of the
state can be used for tyranny.'[26]

This then is another way of preaching on Jesus' healing the demonic, which does justice to what the epistle to the Ephesians describes as wrestling not against flesh and blood but against principalities and powers. Newbigin concludes:

> The principalities and powers are realities. We may not be able to visualize them, to locate them, or to say exactly what they are. But we are foolish if we pretend that they do not exist. Certainly one cannot read the Gospels without recognizing that the ministry of Jesus from beginning to end was a mighty spiritual battle with powers which are not simply human frailties, errors, diseases, or sins.[27]

5

Conclusion

We have looked at various issues relating to preaching about healing and have examined four models which can be utilized for preaching the Gospel healing texts. They are not all mutually exclusive and indeed I will argue in a moment that all are required if a full panoply of truth, as far as we can know it, is to be maintained. We have also seen where the application of these models to two of the more controversial issues in healing leads us. In this final chapter I summarize the insights and discoveries thrown up by this study, which I hope will help preachers to speak honestly and faithfully about healing when they use the healing stories in the Gospels today.

'To preach and to heal'

In this study we have noted from the outset that in Jesus' own ministry and in his apostolic charges to the 12 and the 72 the healing of the sick is always subordinated to the proclamation of the message (Matthew 9.35 and 10.7f.). The healings and exorcisms of Jesus function as important proclamations of the kingdom. They are inextricably linked with his preaching of the gospel of the kingdom of God and are not to be seen as all-important features in themselves. Some so-called 'faith healers' or 'spiritual healers' need reminding of this.

Given the extent of the healing narratives in the Gospels and the frequency, therefore, with which these stories occur in church lectionaries for preaching purposes, we can hardly avoid preaching regularly about healing miracles. The problem, however, as we have seen is that healing is a very untidy subject. There are no straightforward answers. That is why Tull cautions:

> The preacher is to assist the individual church member in formulating a theology that is consistent with the gospel while being able to withstand the tough tests of life. It is not acceptable to preach positive platitudes or offer trite answers to life's profound tragedies. It is not acceptable to escape existential questions with a simple pastoral instruction to embrace everything on faith or to promote the false notion that somehow every tragedy is God's will.[1]

There are glaring inconsistencies, as well as much mystery, in healing. I recall an occasion some years ago when I attended a 'Signs and Wonders' conference run by John Wimber. After preaching about healing he asked people to raise their hands if they needed to receive healing. He then asked those near such a person to gather round and pray for them. I happened to find myself in a group of six others praying for a young man who had lost the feeling in his little finger. As I stood beside him I could not help but reflect on the inconsistency of six of us praying for God to bring back the feeling in this man's little finger, while God himself was apparently failing to lift a finger to help people with serious life-threatening illnesses who prayed to him day and night.

We have to face the fact that, although many people bear witness to God's healing power in their lives and rejoice in it, there are also many others in the world today who sadly do not experience healing, who are not cured of their disabilities when they seek God's help. Furthermore, when we look at people with chronic age-related conditions we ask questions about our own finitude and fragility: 'if they are suffering like this today, what can prevent this from happening to me tomorrow?' 'For the Christian healing ministry to remain authentic, it must come to terms with the fact that some people are not healed, others suffer greatly, many are disabled, and all grow old and will one day die. We need a theology that takes into account the reality of death.'[2] All these tensions will be reflected in our preaching about healing and through which we have to bring messages of hope. 'Perfect health is as unlikely as perfect living, but that doesn't mean we should not expect God to give us his healing grace when it is his will to do so.'[3]

I now wish to critique the four models previously identified before making suggestions as to how these ways of preaching might be held together. Finally, I conclude this study with a look at the eschatological dimension.

Literal versus liberal

The purpose of the evangelists in relating the miracles in the Gospels was to testify to the Lordship of Christ and reveal the presence of the victorious kingdom of God. They were not proofs of Jesus' divinity but were nevertheless written so 'that you may come to believe that

Jesus is the Messiah, the Son of God' (John 20.31). Jesus did not perform miracles for the sake of it, but out of pity and compassion for the sake of the kingdom of God and in the context of faith. Faith was an important ingredient in the miracles – he called for faith, healed in response to it, was limited by lack of it and in John's Gospel his miracles are signs to which the proper response is faith.

Literalists (though not only literalists) will wish to affirm the truth of the healing miracles and the role faith plays in them. Certainly the general evidence for Jesus performing cures is very strong. 'Many scholars from widely different backgrounds now accept that Jesus did remarkable "mighty works".'[4] The crucial question is: 'What implications do these Gospel healing texts have for us today?' How do we interpret these healing narratives for homiletics? Goldingay states: 'Disagreements about the present relevance of some stories (e.g. [...] the use in charismatic renewal circles of stories from the Gospels and Acts about healing [...]) are sometimes disagreements about whether these stories relate solely "events on which the faith is based" or also offer paradigms of how God may act now or of how we should act now.'[5]

There is certainly an attractive simplicity in the literalist view that Jesus sent out his disciples to preach and to heal and that the Church continues his healing ministry, therefore we should expect miracles today (Mark 6.7–13; 16.17–20). This view holds that there is a direct line between Jesus' practice and contemporary healing. Jesus is the model healer *par excellence*, a paradigm for believers to emulate today rather than a unique phenomenon of his day. But as Wenham and Walton point out: 'The New Testament gives the impression that Jesus and his miracles (culminating in his resurrection) are unparalleled in scope and power. The church continues that work in what we might call a lower key (though John 14.12 might suggest otherwise).'[6] The greater works referred to in John 14 must mean the greater geographical opportunities the disciples had of gathering converts into the Church, rather than their performing greater healings than Jesus which is clearly not the case (unless one sees in the advance of medical science the Spirit of Jesus behind the conquest of disease).

When preaching about healing we need to come to terms with the limited success rate of contemporary healing ministries in the Church. There is a marked contrast between Jesus' healing ministry and that of contemporary believers. This leads us to ask the question: 'Is there a general imperative to heal the sick?' The report *A Time to Heal* suggests there is: 'Healing the sick is a gospel imperative along with preaching and teaching.'[7] Buchanan, however, states: 'My own reading of the New Testament, alongside the realities of Christian history and of present-day suffering, leads me to qualify that quotation strongly; and thus to be hesitant about any "gospel imperative" to heal the sick.'[8]

In addition to the crucial question as to whether Jesus is our model for ministry in all respects, the critical question that divides literalists and liberals is this: 'How does God act in relation to his universe?' If we can know the answer to this we will know better how to preach about healing. Does God act directly by controlling the

course of events, as literalists think he does, or does he
allow the universe to run its natural course as many liberals would claim? Alternatively, is it just that God exer-
cises great reserve in communicating with us to protect
human freedom – a kind of 'hide and seek' God whom
we keep losing and finding? Hacker asks:

> Does he, for example, as has been claimed, find parking
> places for harassed clergymen in answer to prayer, or
> washing machines for couples with no money starting a
> Christian community in their home? Alternatively does he
> leave his universe to run itself most of the time, only inter-
> rupting with an occasional miracle? Or does he not even
> do that, and work through 'normal channels' all the time,
> influencing events only through such things as the
> thoughts and choices of men and women, and the desire
> he has put into our hearts for a better world? The short
> answer is of course that we do not know.[9]

Are healings, for example, really suspensions of the
natural laws of nature, or are they more a speeding up of
nature's own healing processes? It is because many
agree that we do not know the answers to these kinds of
questions that they take refuge in models of preaching
other than the literalist or liberal approach by resorting
to metaphorical/spiritual or social/community models.

A helpful way forward when looking at the miraculous
is given by Wright in his discussion of the various Greek
words which come closest to 'miracle'. He states:

> These words do not carry, as the English word 'miracle'
> has sometimes done, overtones of invasion from another
> world, or from outer space. They indicate, rather, that
> something has happened, *within* what we would call the
> 'natural' world, which is not what would have been

anticipated, and which seems to provide evidence for the active presence of an authority, a power, at work, not invading the created order as an alien force, but rather enabling it to be more truly itself.[10]

Perhaps the development of this approach is a way through the literal versus liberal divide. Certainly the idea of a God who sometimes intervenes in the world to work miracles can imply that he has previously been absent from it, when in fact he is already present everywhere as the creator who causes everything to exist.

Metaphorical/spiritual model

What potentialities and pitfalls does this model provide for us in our preaching? Concern has already been expressed about the effects preachers using this model have on disabled people today. Preaching metaphorically or spiritually can be oppressive to disabled people, particularly where physical disability is equated with sin, lack of faith or spiritual resistance to God. So for example with blindness in the story of Bartimaeus (Mark 10.46–52), while a literal reading will emphasize the possibility of cure through faith, a metaphorical reading may portray his blindness as symbolizing a spiritual inability to see (i.e. understand). That is why some would opt for preaching a social reading of this story, whereby Jesus is attentive to his cries while everyone else is trying to shut him up. This reading of the situation would draw attention to the persistence of Bartimaeus and of Jesus affording him his dignity and integrating him back into the community.

I believe, however, that Black goes too far in ruling out a metaphorical approach because of sensitivity to the disabled. In going to such lengths to avoid giving distress to the disabled in our preaching, are we not sometimes going against the Gospel authors' intent? Fuller, in discussing the spiritual interpretation of the miracles, states:

> In the oral tradition the healings of the blind are actually physical miracles, and while Mark also takes it for granted that they are so, that does not prevent him from giving them a further symbolic or spiritual meaning. This he does by placing the cure of the blind man of Bethsaida just before the opening of the disciples' eyes to Jesus' Messiahship at Caesarea Philippi, and blind Bartimaeus after the opening of their eyes to the necessity of the cross at the transfiguration. And this spiritual or symbolic significance of the blindness is clinched at 8.18 ['Do you have eyes and fail to see?'].[11]

It is to Black's credit that she wishes to make preachers more aware of the sensitivities of disabled people to such metaphorical/spiritual interpretations. But disabled people are aware that their disability *is* a disability. Equating *blindness* with sin, for example, is not the same as equating *blackness* with sin, which *is* oppressive to black people. It may *not* be oppressive to blind people to hear their blindness equated with being unable to see God, especially if the preacher sympathetically describes what it must be like to be physically blind when making the link. Blind people may in fact be pleased that their visual impairment might be used to assist themselves and others to experience and *see* spiritual truths. We have to be careful not to rule out preaching metaphorically on such issues when the Gospel writer is clearly encouraging us to do so, for there can be spiritual lessons to be learnt through this approach.

Social/community model

Can this model help us in finding a way forward in preaching about healing? It is right to be concerned about the immense harm that has been caused by insensitive preachers who peddle false hopes by conveying unrealistic expectations of healing from the Gospel stories. There are many conditions for which no physical recovery is normally possible no matter how much faith one has. Black, therefore, believes that the only credible way to preach the healing texts today is by utilizing a social model and this is what she opts for. This social/community dimension of the Gospel healing miracles is an important aspect which is often overlooked in preaching the healing texts and Black is right to draw attention to it. As Wenham and Walton state: 'Often the social and the physical go together: leprosy and some forms of demon possession cut the victim off from society, and other conditions force the ill person into poverty and begging.'[12] Wright goes further and points out that these people were being reintegrated into the worshipping community: 'The effect of these cures, therefore, was not merely to bring physical healing; not merely to give humans, within a far less individualistic society than our modern western one, a renewed sense of community membership; but to reconstitute those healed as members of the people of Israel's god.'[13]

The social/community transformation that Black extols is, however, dependent upon the physical transformation that takes place in Gospel healing stories. Black in laying stress on the social dimension unfortunately appears to play down this physical aspect. In highlighting the love shown by Jesus to the afflicted, she does not seem to give sufficient recognition to the power of Jesus which enabled that love to be effective. Utilizing this model on its own, therefore, is insufficient for preaching the Gospel healing stories, for it does not do justice to the physical dimension of healing.

An analogy

We have looked at four different ways of preaching about healing. Is any one particular model better than another for preaching the Gospel healing texts? Which model a preacher utilizes is likely to depend on his or her theological perspective. They are not all mutually exclusive of course. It is possible to base a sermon on a literal or liberal model and yet incorporate elements, for example, of the metaphorical/spiritual or social/community within it. I suspect, however, that preachers at churches in a particular theological tradition will tend to consistently adopt one particular model. A charismatic church is more likely to utilize a literal model which looks for the healings in the Gospels to be replicated today, while a non-charismatic evangelical church is likely to adopt a metaphorical/spiritual model (as we have seen with two All Souls, Langham Place sermons quoted in Chapter 4). My argument is that all these models are required, if a full panoply of truth as far as we can know and understand it is to be maintained.

I wish to use the analogy of the various traditions within the Christian Church to explore this possibility. St Marylebone Parish Church in Central London, where I am the Rector, has as its neighbours a number of churches whose traditions are all very different. There is All Souls, Langham Place, a conservative evangelical teaching church with a national/international Bible ministry; 250 yards from it is All Saints, Margaret Street, well known nationally as the great Anglo-Catholic 'shrine' of the Church of England with its ceremonial splendour and sacramental ministry *par excellence*. (Similarly, nearby is the Roman Catholic 'shrine' of St James, Spanish Place.) The next parish to St Marylebone going westwards has an Anglican church which has been taken over by a former church plant from Holy Trinity, Brompton with 800 Christians in the charismatic tradition, with its emphasis on informal worship and ministering in the power and gifts of the Holy Spirit. At the other end of Marylebone High Street is the West London Mission Methodist Church in the liberal theological tradition, made famous by Lord Soper, which has an extensive social and community programme including a day centre for the homeless. A stranger to the Christian religion going into each of these churches expecting some consistency in worship, doctrine, practice and outreach may well wonder whether they represent the same religion. Yet collectively these churches bear witness to the Christian gospel in a way that is bigger than any of them individually. They may, and probably do, think that their way of doing things is the right way, but it is not the only way and although they may not admit it each has only a partial vision of the whole. The tragedy is that Christianity has become compartmentalized. Sacramentalists go one way for channels of grace, charismatics collect elsewhere to minister in the Spirit and so on, but no one particular tradition has a complete hold of the truth. My hope is that many individual churches may come to embrace the whole spectrum of Christian experience within each of their own four walls. It would certainly assist the task of Christian unity.

Let us now apply this analogy to the task before us of looking at the four different ways of preaching about healing that have been identified. Is it possible within one sermon on a Gospel healing text to bring together these four different models in order to gain a wider spectrum of understanding of Christian truth, similar to the analogous situation of the Church? The big stumbling block is the literal/liberal divide, but need it necessarily be so? Let us take as an example the story referred to earlier of the Gadarene demoniac who lived among the tombs and revisit the text in Luke 8.26–39 and its parallels in Mark 5.1–20 and Matthew 8.28–34 utilizing suggestions already made.

Preaching the Gadarene demoniac

The starting point for such a sermon could either be a liberal perspective or a literalist perspective, which way round does not really matter. A literalist preacher will probably wish to lead with a liberal model in order to feel that they were knocking it down, and vice versa with the liberal preacher. Nevertheless, the congregation can be told that there are two ways of looking at demon possession in this text.

A literal reading would take the narrative as it stands and tell the story as it is, possibly utilizing a narrative preaching style. The demonic is real. People can become possessed or oppressed by demons from which they need exorcizing or deliverance ministry, as was the case with this man. This narrative tells of an evil that has taken control of this man's life without his consent and which threatens destruction. He lives among the tombs, an appropriate dwelling place for someone taken over by the power of evil. Jesus liberates him and sends the demons into a herd of pigs who plunge to their death. As a result of Jesus' action the man is left clothed and in his right mind. The not unnatural reaction of the other people in the story is to be afraid, which results in them asking Jesus to leave the district. Some people today may be demonized or oppressed by evil spirits like this demoniac. The literalist will probably wish to cite contemporary examples that abound in charismatic testimonies of Jesus delivering people from evil and from the clutches of the evil one, who opposes God's power and spreads sin and sickness.

A liberal reading, however, in retelling the story, will demythologize the scriptural text and reinterpret what the demonic stands for. In this story Jesus adopted the thought forms of his day which believed in demon possession. A liberal interpretation may seek to equate demonic behaviour with mental illness today. Certain forms of it may cause an individual to hear voices that instruct the individual what to say or do. Jesus' ministry to the demoniac left him clothed and in his right mind. If the pig story has any credibility as fact, it was merely the case that the rantings of the insane man caused the pigs to take fright and plunge to their death. There is no objective reality to the possession aspect, or any such link between evil spirits and sickness. It is a product of a world view that no longer has a place in modern society. But mental illness is very much a reality and the liberal model will dwell on ways in which healing can be brought to bear upon it through medical and spiritual means.

There seems to me no good reason why the literal and liberal models should not be placed side by side in a sermon and the hearers left to decide for themselves which rings true in their own experience. The literalist, of course, will be bound by the authority of the biblical text and will not wish to be seen compromising it. The liberal, however, while not necessarily denying the authority of the text (only reinterpreting it differently) will wish to apply the understanding of twentieth-century medical science to this story and not to be seen inhabiting some outdated world view. Jesus' understanding was conditioned by the beliefs prevalent at that time.

Both these positions need to come to terms with the fact, however, that we do not know whether evil spirits have any objective reality. Each position thinks it knows but it cannot. The literalist will be happy to use this biblical story as it stands with its language and imagery, for the spiritual battle against the forces of evil is very real indeed. However, the liberal will seek to trace such evil ultimately to natural causes. It seems sensible, therefore, if one is not to be prejudiced, to provide in a sermon both options for the hearer, because there will always be differences of opinion as to whether evil spirits exist.

The sermon can now move on to the third model, that of the metaphorical/spiritual, in a way that can unite literalist and liberal alike and also not fall foul of the criticism that this model is oppressive to persons with disabilities. In the story of the Gadarene demoniac this approach will deal with the man's self-destructive impulse and of his being rescued and delivered from the power of evil. It may focus on the psychological demons and addictions of various kinds that can grip us and on the power of Christ to liberate us. God's intention is for us to be at home, clothed and in our right mind. Further metaphorical or spiritual connections can be made, such as those mentioned earlier centring on the 'legion' of demons or the destruction of the pigs. The pigs plunging to their death can be seen as a sign of the ultimately self-destructive nature of evil. This model may also draw out feelings of helplessness and hopelessness in the face of evil with which the hearer can identify, such as the hijacking of an aeroplane by terrorists.

Finally, the sermon could conclude with the fourth social/community model. Evil makes human community impossible. The evil spirits drove this man away from the community. Alienated from family and friends he lived alone among the tombs separated from normal human relationships, which is one of the most harmful consequences of the presence of evil. Many today with mental illness are alienated from family and friends and some are shut away in mental institutions. Jesus' compassion reaches those who live in despair on the very fringes of society. Relationships which have been destroyed by evil are restored, as Jesus returns them to the homes and communities from which they came. The fear factor (Luke 8.37) may also be addressed as previously indicated.

In concluding this story, the 'healing and evangelism' issue can be picked up. Jesus said to the man: 'Return to your home, and declare how much God has done for you.' Not only does he enable the man to regain control of his own life, but Jesus gives him the task of going back home to preach the good news. Trusting the mentally ill with responsibility and giving them some meaning to their lives as part of the community is important. In this case the man becomes a missionary to his own community. He receives what is the Gospel's first commission to proclaim what God has done for him through Jesus. He is a pattern for evangelism, for he is instructed to tell his own story. He becomes a *preacher* about healing, which is a fitting example on which to conclude a study on preaching and healing. Jesus has the final word, for although those in the town and surrounding countryside ask him to leave the district, the testimony to him remains, for Jesus leaves one of their own to witness to them. Such a witness is the responsibility of all those whose lives have been touched in some way by Jesus.

Here then is a way forward, I believe, in preaching honestly and faithfully about healing today, which bases a sermon on all the four ways of preaching identified in Chapter 3 and which can also bring in issues identified in Chapter 2. The absence of one or more of these four models will result in not telling 'the truth, the whole truth and nothing but the truth'. So, for example, if a liberal model is excluded, use of the literal model will preach faithfully on the text, but will it be honest? Likewise a liberal model may be honest, but if the literal is excluded will it be faithful to the text? And if the metaphorical or community models are missing will not certain important spiritual or social lessons be lost?

Dick's story

I want to use the story of Dick as an example of how we might use the experience of a disabled (differently abled) person to preach a short homily on healing, encapsulating the four different ways of preaching about healing that I have identified: literal, liberal, metaphorical/spiritual and social/community.

In 1974 Dick had just graduated from Cambridge University. One day Dick, his friend and their girlfriends were on a car journey. His friend was driving when they had a terrible accident and Dick was thrown from the car down an embankment. At the age of 24 he was in a coma for a year. He was blind for 15 months, when suddenly his sight began to be restored. He was unable to speak and to this day communication remains difficult. He is hemiplegic, partially paralysed on the right side. It is a moving sight to see Dick, now in his early fifties, being helped to the communion rail by his 85-year-old mother to receive communion. Over the years many prayers have been offered for Dick and his family, no doubt with particular intensity during those first two years following the accident. Dick has also been to healing services over the years.

For his parents Dick's return to consciousness after a year, followed by the restoration of his sight, were nothing short of a miracle and an answer to their prayers. Here was an example of a God who brings people back to life again and who gives recovery of sight to the blind. The promises of Jesus in the Gospels are literally fulfilled. On one occasion Dick exhibited some of his own paintings in a church, with these words underneath: 'God walked beside me, sometimes he carried me.'

But liberal questioning is never far away for those who are suspicious of any kind of supernatural miraculous healing, and who will want to question Gospel healing stories when making pastoral connections with those who suffer today. Was not this partial recovery achieved by natural and medical means? If it was an example of a direct intervention by God, why was the recovery not completed? Why leave a person to suffer disability for all those years and place intolerable burdens upon the family? When Dick was first admitted to hospital following his accident, his mother asked the Ward Sister for a key to the chapel. The Sister replied: 'You want to be careful what you are praying for, because he's going to be a cabbage, you know.' His mother said: 'I'm just praying that God will help me cope with whatever I have to deal with.'

For Dick and his family, however, there have been spiritual blessings to compensate. Often weary and carrying heavy burdens they have found from time to time the '*rest*' that Jesus promised (Matthew 11.28) in the middle of their '*wrestle*' with life. They have found God's strength in their weakness, and like the man born blind (John 9.1–3) God's works have been revealed through Dick's life. He has been an inspiration and spiritual blessing to us all. He never leaves church without struggling to utter the word 'Alleluia'. One of Dick's great loves is to read, albeit slowly. Such is his gratitude to God for his sight being restored which has enabled him to read, that on two occasions he has given generously for the purchase of Bibles for children in church. Metaphorically, his restoration of sight has also helped him to see life in other ways that we cannot, not least in thankfulness for life itself. His story reminds us of the thankfulness of one of the ten lepers healed by Jesus (Luke 17.15), in contrast to the other nine who took their restoration for granted. Dick's mother feels that whenever people see Dick it helps them also to be thankful.

Finally, there are social/community implications in this story. I mentioned in discussing the healing of the paralytic in Mark 2 how important disabled access is in allowing those with disabilities to gain entry into the meeting place of the faith community. Dick's family are Methodists and his father attends a Methodist church. Dick and his mother come to St Marylebone, however, because the disabled access is easier. It has been wonderful to see how, with the right care and support from others, Dick has been able to be reintegrated back into the life of the community, when he could so easily have been marginalized as a result of his disability. Dick is a contented person and few things frustrate him. One thing that makes him angry, however, is when he is out with his parents and they meet someone who asks his parents how Dick is rather than asking Dick himself.

Yet Dick can be understood with the help of some lip-reading by his mother. Social acceptance is of vital importance.

There is much to learn from Dick's experience of life, as well as heart-searching questions of faith to be considered. A total picture requires all four models to be utilized in telling his story, if we are to preach honestly and faithfully about healing today. The narrative preaching of Gospel healing miracles can incorporate stories like Dick's, either by focusing primarily on the biblical story and alluding to such healing experiences today, or by focusing on the contemporary story and alluding to the biblical text(s). Dick's story shows how a combination of models is not only useful but necessary when speaking of healing. The models can also be applied to the issues identified earlier in this book, such as the evidence for healing, faith in relation to healing and the use or otherwise of such healing stories in evangelism.

The eschatological dimension

We have come, then, to the end of this study on how we can use the healing stories in the Gospels to preach honestly and faithfully about healing today. We have taken account of the various issues involved in healing and identified four models or ways of preaching about healing, applying them to two particularly controversial issues. I have offered a path forward by way of analogy and example for preaching comprehensively about healing. However, an important dimension of preaching about healing that needs some comment in closing is the eschatological dimension, that expression of Christian hope concerning the end of life in its present form.

It is one of life's paradoxes that we do not start to live fully until we have also faced up to death. Following an investigation into the role of religion in health, the National Institute of Healthcare Research in America published in June 2000 the results of medical research which showed that regular churchgoers live on average seven years longer than other people. Christians like everyone else, however, have to face up to sickness and death at some stage. That is a very hard thing to do and sometimes can be quite traumatic.

A couple of years ago I called to see a man in the Harley Street Clinic, who told me his story. He had been hospitalized 16 times with pancreatic cancer between 1989 and 1992 in Germany where he came from. In 1997 he was in hospital again with a further spread of the disease. He told me that while undergoing chemotherapy he was given the news that his wife and three children, aged 19 months, 5 years and 7 years, had been killed in a car accident. He was now alone and bereft. In Germany he was informed that he had between 8 and 12 months to live and should go into a hospice. As he put it, he knew that if he went into a hospice the doors would close behind him and he would never come out. It would be his coffin, he said, and his freedom to live would be lost. So he went to Cork in Southern Ireland. In his mind he thought that if he left his homeland he would leave his cancer behind. Alas, he was taken ill in Ireland. He realized he was living a fantasy, but refused to go home and take up his place in a hospice. He wanted his freedom. He therefore went to Canterbury to visit a friend, but became more ill and ended up in the

Harley Street Clinic utterly desolate, from where he called me to have a chat to break his loneliness. He now had to come to terms with the fact that he would have to return home and enter a hospice to prepare for his death.

McGrath comments that hospitals are powerful reminders and symbols of human frailty and mortality, tokens of our vulnerability. Funerals, he notes, are intended to remind those present that they are still alive – for the time being. He states:

> God is obliged to bring about the funeral of a great myth – the myth of our personal immortality and the permanence of the world. These things must pass, and we shall pass with them. But God will live on – and so can we, in union with him. But not if we cling steadfastly to the world and its values. Suffering and the death of those we know and love break down the pretence of human permanence. We do not want to admit our own mortality. We find it deeply threatening to accept that the world and all whom we love will one day pass beyond our grasp. It is so much more reassuring to believe that we and the world will go on forever – that we will be able to hold on to all the glittering prizes which we win during life. But the reality is very different. Suffering strips away our illusions of immortality. It causes anxiety to rear its ugly, yet revealing, head. It batters down the gates of the citadel of illusions. It confronts us with the harsh facts of life. And it makes us ask those hard questions which have the power to erode falsehood and propel us away from the false security and transient rewards of the world towards our loving God.[14]

It is this wrestling with the hard questions about suffering and what lies beyond that our preaching needs to address. 'Our eyes need to be lifted to catch a glimpse of another country; to hear its music.'[15] It is this future dimension that writers like Black can neglect. In stressing that the Gospel healing texts offer no guarantee or promise of total healing now, they can omit to point forward to the promise and future hope that these texts do hold out for complete healing in God's ultimate plan.

In the opening chapter of this book we saw how the central theme of Jesus' message was the preaching of the kingdom of God. Although this kingdom has invaded human history in the person and mission of Jesus, the consummation of God's kingly rule will be beyond history in the life of the age to come, when creation will be restored and suffering and evil are finally defeated. Jesus, and indeed that first generation of Christians, interpreted his death and resurrection as the beginning of that process. Glimpses of this future kingdom can be seen in Jesus' healing miracles and exorcisms. They are signs of the kingdom but not its total embodiment.

Christians need to hold a balance between a 'realized eschatology' which centres upon the transformation of life now within present history and which can be seen in the kingdom of God being present in the healings of Jesus, and a 'futurist eschatology' which emphasizes the radical transformation that will take place at the end of history. We need to hold a balance between these two perspectives in the tension of the already/not yet that is part of the Christian experience of salvation.

Healing is inherent in Christianity, as we see from the ministry of Jesus, and if we accept his bodily resurrection from the dead we can also accept that God can be interventionist in some sense, both now and in the future. Our preaching needs to contain an eschatological dimension which considers our future hope, for the healings of Jesus point forward to the ultimate goal of a restored humanity and creation. They are foretastes of a new order to come. If God created us he can recreate us. At present 'we are tied to this earth by sin, like gravity'[16] and suffering holds us in its grip. But the New Testament promises an end to suffering with the final coming of the kingdom of God when there will be a new heaven and a new earth in which suffering and pain will be a thing of the past, for we will be enfolded in the love of God in a life that is eternal. This vision of a world transformed is described in Romans 8.19–23 and Revelation 21.1–4.

If Jesus and the Gospel evangelists saw the miracles of healing as forward signs, foretastes of God's kingdom, then it makes sense for us to see healing in that light today as well. This means that there will always be an incompleteness to healing which hints at a greater fulfilment to come. We shall all die in various states of unwholeness: surely there must be more to hope for in the future? Polkinghorne comments: 'The workings of divine grace will not only involve healing of disability and the restoration of decay, but it may also be expected to begin its work within all of us, for we shall all need God's sanctifying and redeeming touch beyond what we have already experienced in this world.'[17]

What ground is there for the hope that our lives will not end in death, or that the world will not end in futility as science predicts? The real ground for human expectation of a destiny beyond death lies in trust in the everlasting faithfulness and steadfast love of God. Would a loving God create us, only to drop us out of existence

after a few years and thereby render human life mean-
ingless? This loving faithfulness is also testified to by the
resurrection of Jesus Christ, which provides the fore-
taste and guarantee that God will re-embody us in some
future environment. This future destiny must allow continuity of our own identities (with surely further room
for growth and development), yet also discontinuity in
that we shall be free from sickness, suffering and mortality. 'If human beings are creatures loved by their
Creator, they must have a destiny beyond their deaths.
Every generation must participate equally in that
destiny, in which it will receive the healing of its hurts
and the restoration of its integrity.'[18]

Polkinghorne draws attention to the intuitive hope
that lies deep within each one of us: 'Despite the
strangeness, bitterness, incompleteness of this present
life, human beings frequently do not give way to
despair. In the human heart there is something that cor-
responds to the conviction expressed so powerfully by
the great fourteenth-century mystic, Mother Julian of
Norwich, that in the end "all shall be well and all
manner of things shall be well".'[19] It is this conviction
that forms the basis of this book and lies at the heart of
the Gospel preached with the hope of healing.

Notes

Chapter 1: Introduction

1 Black, K., *A Healing Homiletic*. Abingdon Press, Nashville, 1996, p. 157.
2 *Miracles*. Carlton TV, 18.6.2001.
3 *Church Times*. 27.4.2001.
4 Wright, T., *Jesus and the Victory of God*. SPCK, London, 1996, p. 186.
5 See Wright, *Jesus and the Victory of God*, p. 191.
6 Meier, J., *A Marginal Jew*. Vol. 2. Doubleday, New York, 1994, p. 349.
7 Meier, *A Marginal Jew*, Vol. 2, p. 350.
8 Meier, *A Marginal Jew*, Vol. 2, p. 450.
9 Ladd, G., *The Presence of the Future*. Eerdmans, Michigan, 1974, p. 218.
10 Iremonger, F. A., *William Temple*. Oxford University Press, Oxford, 1948, p. 612.
11 *A Time to Heal* – A report on the Healing Ministry for the House of Bishops of the General Synod of the Church of England. Church House Publishing, London, 2000, p. 209.
12 *A Time to Heal*, p. xiii.
13 Warrington, K., *Jesus the Healer. Paradigm or Unique Phenomenon?* Paternoster Press, Carlisle, 2000, pp. ix–x.

Chapter 2: Issues in healing

1 *A Time to Heal*, p. 129.
2 Jarrett-Kerr, 'Scott Holland: drains and the Incarnation', *The Times*. 5.2.1983.
3 Leach, K., *True God*. Sheldon Press, London, 1985, p. 384.
4 *A Time to Heal*, p. 278.
5 *Church Times*. 13.2.1981.
6 MacNutt, F., *The Power to Heal*. Ave Maria Press, Notre Dame, 1977, p. 155: italics original.
7 Tull, J., *Why, God, Why? Sermons on the Problem of Pain*. Abingdon Press, Nashville, 1996, p. 8.
8 Wimber, J., *Power Healing*. Hodder & Stoughton, London, 1986, p. 58.
9 See Hick, J., *Evil and the God of Love*. Collins, Glasgow, 1966, pp. 262f.
10 Polkinghorne, J., *Science and Theology*. SPCK, London, 1998, p. 94.
11 Polkinghorne, *Science and Theology*, p. 94.
12 Ward, K., *God, Faith and the New Millennium*. One World, Oxford, 1998, p. 102.
13 Black, *A Healing Homiletic*, p. 42.
14 Black, *A Healing Homiletic*, p. 36.
15 Petrie, E., *Unleashing the Lion: the Power of God in Health and Healing*. SPCK, London, 2000, p. 166.
16 *A Time to Heal*, p. 22.
17 MacNutt, F., *Healing*. Hodder & Stoughton, London, Revised Edition 1989, p. 108.
18 MacNutt, *Healing*, p. 136.
19 *A Time to Heal*, p. 222.
20 Warrington, *Jesus the Healer*, p. 18.
21 Black, *A Healing Homiletic*, p. 84.
22 Black, *A Healing Homiletic*, p. 26.
23 Buchanan, C., *Services for Wholeness and Healing*. Grove Books, Cambridge, 2000, p. 12.

24 *A Time to Heal*, p. 232.
25 Wimber, *Power Healing*, p. 172.
26 *A Time to Heal*, p. 23.
27 *A Time to Heal*, pp. 25–26.
28 Parker, R. and Lawrence, R., *Healing and Evangelism*. SPCK, London, 1996, p. 34.
29 Wimber, *Power Healing*, p. 60.
30 *A Time to Heal*, p. xiii.
31 Skinner, S., *Evangelism and Healing*. Grove Books, Cambridge, 1995, p. 12.
32 Skinner, *Evangelism and Healing*, p. 12.
33 Hacker, G., *The Healing Stream*. Darton, Longman & Todd, London, 1998, p. 60.
34 May, P., 'My view of the healing ministry', *Healing and Wholeness*. July 1995, pp. 42–43.
35 Wimber, *Power Healing*, p. 54.
36 Wimber, *Power Healing*, p. 57.
37 Black, *A Healing Homiletic*, pp. 21–22.
38 Wimber, *Power Healing*, p. 81.
39 MacNutt, *Healing*, p. 169.
40 Lawrence, R., *Finding Hope and Healing through the Bible*. SPCK, London, 2000, p. 105.
41 *A Time to Heal*, p. 247.
42 MacNutt, *Healing*, p. 87.
43 *A Time to Heal*, p. 245.
44 *A Time to Heal*, p. 224.
45 Hacker, *The Healing Stream*, p. 117.
46 Hacker, *The Healing Stream*, p. 119.
47 Black, *A Healing Homiletic*, p. 119.
48 Black, *A Healing Homiletic*, p. 112: italics original.
49 *A Time to Heal*, p. 224.
50 Wimber, *Power Healing*, p. 116: italics original.
51 Percy, M., *Words, Wonders and Power*. SPCK, London, 1996, p. 55.
52 Wimber, *Power Healing*, p. 122.
53 Black, *A Healing Homiletic*, p. 45.

54 *A Time to Heal*, p. 172.
55 *A Time to Heal*, p. 253.
56 Percy, *Words, Wonders and Power*, p. 67.
57 Percy, *Words, Wonders and Power*, p. 71.
58 MacNutt, *Healing*, p. 152.
59 Percy, *Words, Wonders and Power*, p. 58.
60 Parker, R., Fraser, D. and Rivers, D., *In Search of Whole-ness*. St John's Extension Studies, Nottingham, 2000, p. 96.
61 *A Time to Heal*, p. 216.
62 MacNutt, *Healing*, p. 33.
63 MacNutt, *Healing*, p. 35.
64 MacNutt, *The Power to Heal*, p. 27: italics original.
65 *A Time to Heal*, p. 229.
66 *A Time to Heal*, p. 220.
67 Hacker, *The Healing Stream*, pp. 48–49.
68 *A Time to Heal*, p. 143.
69 Hacker, *The Healing Stream*, p. 49.

Chapter 3: Ways of preaching Gospel healing stories

1 MacNutt, *Healing*, p. 63.
2 MacNutt, *The Power to Heal*, pp. 126–127.
3 MacNutt, *Healing*, p. 58.
4 Black, *A Healing Homiletic*, p. 44.
5 Black, *A Healing Homiletic*, pp. 44–45.
6 Black, *A Healing Homiletic*, p. 43.
7 *A Time to Heal*, p. 2.
8 Hacker, *The Healing Stream*, p. 116.
9 MacNutt, *Healing*, p. 47.
10 Black, *A Healing Homiletic*, p. 43.
11 Black, *A Healing Homiletic*, p. 55.
12 Black, *A Healing Homiletic*, p. 56.
13 Black, *A Healing Homiletic*, p. 121: italics original.
14 Hacker, *The Healing Stream*, p. 173.
15 MacNutt, *Healing*, p. 161.

Chapter 4: Preaching controversial issues

1 Hacker, *The Healing Stream*, p. 115.
2 Black, *A Healing Homiletic*, p. 117.
3 Hooker, M., *The Gospel According to St Mark*. A. & C. Black, London, 1991, pp. 85–86.
4 Hacker, *The Healing Stream*, p. 123.
5 Tice, R., *Jesus meets a paralytic*. All Souls, Langham Place audio cassette, 16.10.1997.
6 Black, *A Healing Homiletic*, p. 122.
7 *The Times*. 2.9.2000.
8 Wimber, *Power Healing*, p. 120.
9 Percy, *Words, Wonders and Power*, p. 183.
10 MacNutt, *Healing*, p. 220.
11 MacNutt, *Healing*, p. 229.
12 Black, *A Healing Homiletic*, p. 161.
13 Black, *A Healing Homiletic*, p. 162.
14 Newbigin, L., *The Gospel in a Pluralist Society*. SPCK, London, 1989, p. 200.
15 Fuller, R., *Interpreting the Miracles*. SCM, London, 1963, pp. 119–120: italics original.
16 Black, *A Healing Homiletic*, p. 162.
17 Green, M., *I Believe in Satan's Downfall*. Hodder & Stoughton, London, 1981, pp. 19–21.
18 Black, *A Healing Homiletic*, p. 161.
19 Beasley-Murray, G., *Preaching the Gospel from the Gospels*. Epworth Press, London, 1965, p. 68.
20 Williams, P., *For life not death*. All Souls, Langham Place audio cassette, 9.3.2000.
21 Black, *A Healing Homiletic*, pp. 168–169.
22 Black, *A Healing Homiletic*, p. 178.
23 Black, *A Healing Homiletic*, p. 179.
24 Newbigin, *The Gospel in a Pluralist Society*, p. 199.
25 Newbigin, *The Gospel in a Pluralist Society*, p. 207: italics original.
26 Newbigin, *The Gospel in a Pluralist Society*, p. 205.

27 Newbigin, *The Gospel in a Pluralist Society*, p. 210.

Chapter 5: Conclusion

1 Tull, *Why, God, Why?* p. 7.
2 Parker, Fraser and Rivers, *In Search of Wholeness*, p. 18.
3 *A Time to Heal*, p. 231.
4 Wright, *Jesus and the Victory of God*, p. 194.
5 Goldingay, J., *Models for Interpretation of Scripture*. Paternoster Press, Carlisle, 1995, p. 61.
6 Wenham, D. and Walton, S., *Exploring the New Testament*. Vol. 1. SPCK, London, 2001, p. 107.
7 *A Time to Heal*, pp. 50–51.
8 Buchanan, *Services for Wholeness and Healing*, p. 11.
9 Hacker, *The Healing Stream*, p. 117.
10 Wright, *Jesus and the Victory of God*, p. 188: italics original.
11 Fuller, *Interpreting the Miracles*, p. 125.
12 Wenham and Walton, *Exploring the New Testament*. Vol. 1, p. 105.
13 Wright, *Jesus and the Victory of God*, p. 192.
14 McGrath, A., *Why does God allow Suffering?* Hodder & Stoughton, London, 1992, p. 30.
15 McGrath, *Why does God allow Suffering?*, p. 31.
16 McGrath, *Why does God allow Suffering?*, p. 31.
17 Polkinghorne, J., *The God of Hope and the End of the World*. SPCK, London, 2002, pp. 111–112.
18 Polkinghorne, *The God of Hope and the End of the World*, p. 148.
19 Polkinghorne, *The God of Hope and the End of the World*, p. 31.